The Outdoor Girls
At Ocean View

BY

LAURA LEE HOPE

[ZHINGOORA BOOKS]

CONTENTS

CHAPTER I

ANTICIPATIONS

Three girls were strolling down the street, and, as on the occasion when the three fishermen once sailed out to sea, the sun was going down. The golden rays, slanting in from over the western hills that stood back of the little town of Deepdale, struck full in the faces of the maids as they turned a corner, and so bright was the glare that one of them—a tall, willowy lass, with a wealth of fluffy, light hair, turned aside with a cry of annoyance.

"Oh, why can't the sun be nice!" she exclaimed, half-petulantly.

"What do you want it to do, Grace?" asked a vivacious, dark-complexioned sprite next to the complaining one. "Go under a cloud just to suit you?"

"No, my dear, I'm not as fussy as that!"

"Indeed not!" chimed in the third member of the trio, a quiet girl, with thoughtful eyes. "What Grace wants is some nice young fellow to come along with an umbrella, hoist it over her, and invite her in to have—a chocolate soda!"

"Why, Amy Blackford! I'll never speak to you again!" gasped the accused one, blushing vividly, the more so as the rays of the setting sun fell upon her face. "All I said was——"

"Look!" suddenly interrupted the vivacious member of the small party—a party that attracted no little attention, for at the sight of the three pretty girls, strolling arm in arm down the main

5

thoroughfare of the town, more than one person turned for a second look.

"Gracious! What is it?" demanded Grace. "Did you see—some one, Billy?"

"No—something," came the answer from the dark girl with the boyish name, and at a glance you could understand why she was called so. There was such a wholesome, frank and comrade-like quality about her, though she was not at all masculine, that "Billy" just suited.

"Look," she went on. "Isn't that a perfectly gorgeous display of chocolates!" and she indicated the window of a confectionery store just in front of them.

"Oh, I must have some of those!" cried Grace Ford. "Come on in, girls! I'll treat. They're those new bitter-sweet chocolates. I didn't know Borker kept them. I'm simply dying for some!" and with this rather exaggerated statement she fairly pulled her two chums after her into the store.

"Look!" Grace went on, pausing a moment when inside the shop to glance at the chocolate display in the show-window. "Did you ever see anything so—so appetizing?"

"It looks like a display at a picnic candy kitchen," murmured she who had been called Billy.

"Why, Mollie Billette!" reproached Grace Ford. "I think it's perfectly splendid."

"But not appetizing," declared Amy Blackford. "I don't see how you can think of eating any, when it's so near dinner time, Grace."

"We don't have dinner until seven, and it's only five. Besides, I'm not going to eat many—now."

"No, she'll take a box home, and keep them in bed, under her pillow—I know her," put in Mollie, alias Billy. "I slept with her one night and I wondered whether she had lumps of coal, or some kitchen kindling wood between the sheets. But it wasn't—it was chocolates! The box had worked out from under her pillow in the night and——

"Mollie Billette! You promised never to tell that!" pouted Grace. "I don't care. They were hard chocolates, and didn't do any damage."

"No, and they weren't damaged, either," laughed Mollie. "I know we sat up eating them until your mother came in and made us go to sleep. Oh, Grace, you certainly are hopeless when it comes to chocolates!"

A smiling clerk came up to wait on the girls, and while Grace was pointing out what she wanted, the two friends stood aside, talking in low tones.

"Where are you going this summer?" asked Mollie, of Amy.

"I don't know. Henry isn't just sure what he will do—at least, he wasn't the last I talked with him about it. I suppose, though, I shall go wherever Mr. and Mrs. Stonington go, and that is likely to be the mountains, I heard them say. What are your plans, Mollie?"

"About as unsettled as yours. I did want to go to the seashore, but mamma is so afraid of the water for Paul and Dodo. Those children never seem to grow, and half my pleasure is spoiled giving way to them."

"Oh, but they are such sweet dears!" protested Amy.

"Yes, I know, but you ought to live with them a year or so. Did I tell you Paul's latest?"

"I think not."

"Well, he has a rocking-horse, you know, and the other day——"

"Have some," interrupted Grace, thrusting her bag of chocolates between her two girl chums, and thus interrupting Mollie's story. "Don't you want a soda? I've enough change left."

"Soda? Indeed not!" cried Mollie. "And I don't want more than one or two candies, either!" she went on, as she tried to prevent Grace from generously emptying half the bag into her small, gloved hands.

The three girls were laughing and—yes, truth compels me to say they were giggling—when the door of the shop swung open, a girl entered and at the sight of the newcomer the three burst out with:

"Betty!"

"The Little Captain!"

"Betty Nelson, where were you? We've been looking all over for you!"

"Yes, so I heard," was the calm response of the fourth girl, who swung in with a certain vigor and lithesomeness as though she had just come from a game of tennis or basketball. There was a wholesome air of good health about her, a sparkle in her eyes, and a glow in her cheeks that told of life in the open.

"I saw you turn in here," she went on, "and I knew I had plenty of time, as long as I saw Grace with you, so I didn't hurry."

"Oh, I haven't bought so much," declared Grace, with an injured air. "Just because I want some chocolates now and then——"

"Now—and—then!" mocked Betty Nelson, with a laugh. "Better say now—and—always. No, thank you," and with a shake of her head she declined some candy from the bag. "Just had lunch a little while ago. Mother and I ate on the train."

"Where were you?" demanded Mollie. "At the house they said you were out of town, and we thought it strange, as you hadn't said anything about going away, especially as we so recently came back from Florida."

"It was just a little trip, suddenly taken," Betty explained. "Mother and I went down to the shore to select our summer cottage."

"And did you?" asked Mollie, with sparkling eyes.

"We did, and, oh, it's such a darling place!"

"Where?" came the question in a chorus.

"At Ocean View, the prettiest place on the New England coast, I think. Of course it'ssmall, and old fashioned, and all that, but——"

"Oh, how I wish wewere going to some place like that!" exclaimed Mollie.

"So do I," chimed in Grace. "Father talks of Lake Champlain again, and I detest it."

"How about you, Amy?" asked the Little Captain, turning to the quiet girl.

"I haven't heard where we are going."

"Good!" cried Betty. "This is just what I expected. If you haven't any plans, none will have to be—un-made. It makes it so much easier."

"Makes what easier?" demanded Mollie.

"My plan, my dear! Listen, I think it's just the loveliest idea. Mother and I looked at two cottages. One was almost too small, and the other was much too large, until I unfolded my plan to her. Then she saw that it was just right."

"Just right for what?" asked Grace.

"Just right for all us girls to go there and spend the summer. Now don't say a word until you have heard it all!" cautioned Betty, as she saw signs of protest on Amy's face. "You must agree with me—at least for once."

"As if she didn't always have her way!" remarked Mollie.

"We four—the Outdoor Girls—are going toOcean View for the summer!" went on Betty. "We'll have the loveliest, gayest times, for it's the most beautiful beach! And the cottage is a perfect dear—it's just charming. Mother has agreed, so it's all settled. All that remains is to tell your people, and we'll do that right away. Come on!" and leading her friends forth from the candy-shop, Betty really seemed like some little captain marshaling her pretty forces.

"The seashore!" repeated Amy. "Oh, I'm sure I should love it!"

"Of course you would, dear!" exclaimed Betty. "And that's where you—and all of us—are going!"

"Oh, but you are so *sure!*" exclaimed Mollie, in accented tones.

"Oh, but you are so—Frenchy!" half-mocked Betty, with a laugh.

"There! It is all settled! We will spend the Summer at Ocean View! And now come down to my house and we'll talk about it!"

And, filled with delightful anticipations, the four girls strolled down the sun-lit street.

CHAPTER II

INTERRUPTIONS

"Come in, girls! Grace, put your chocolates—what are left of them—over on the mantel. Now sit down, and I'll tell you all about it."

Betty drew forward some easy chairs for her guests, who distributed themselves about the handsome library, in more or less artistic confusion. Betty herself took a hard, uncompromising sort of chair, of teakwood, wonderfully carved by some dead and forgotten Chinese artist. The seat was of red marble, and the back was inlaid with ivory, in the shape of a grinning face.

"Do keep yourself close against it, Betty dear," begged Grace, who sat opposite her friend. "That Chinese face positively hypnotizes me."

"Well, I want you all to be hypnotized into quietness, long enough to listen to me," spoke Betty, with a charmingly commanding air.

Grace Ford, obediently depositing her chocolates on the mantel, save a few which she "sequestered" for use during the talk, had tastefully "draped" herself on a comfortable couch. Mollie, with a mind to color effect, had seated herself in a big chair that had a flame-colored velvet back, against which her blue-black hair showed to advantage (like a poster girl, Betty said), while Amy, like the quiet little mouse which she was, had stolen off into a corner, where she was half-hidden by a palm.

"And, now to begin at the beginning," announced Betty. "Oh, I know you will just love it at Ocean View!" and she gave a little squeal of delight.

"I wish we were as sure of going as you are," murmured Grace, putting out the tip of her red tongue, to absorb a drop of chocolate from a long, slim finger.

"Just you wait," said Betty, half-mysteriously.

And while she is preparing to plunge into the details concerning the new summer plans, I will take just a moment to tell my new readers something about the other books of this series, and give them an idea of the girls themselves.

In "The Outdoor Girls of Deepdale; Or, Camping and Tramping for Fun and Health," the originating idea of the four girls was set forth. They felt that they were spending too much time indoors, and they decided to live more in the glorious open. They felt that they would have better health and more fun in doing this, and events proved that they were right, at least in part.

As for the girls themselves, they were Grace Ford, Mollie Billette, Betty Nelson and Amy Stonington-Blackford, or nee Blackford, if you dislike the hyphen. But that latter form of name does not indicate that Amy was married.

In the opening story Amy's name was Stonington, the ward of John and Sarah Stonington. But there was a mystery in her past, and it was solved when, in addition to unraveling the mystery of a five-hundred-dollar bill, Amy found a long-lost brother, whose name was Henry Blackford.

So Amy's real name was found to be Blackford, though she continued to live with the Stoningtons, and more than half the time her chums called her by the name under which they had known her so long.

Amy was a girl of quiet disposition, and while she had not been altogether happy during the time she was unable to solve the mystery about her identity, when that problem had been cleared up she was of a much brighter disposition. Still, the years of quiet had had their effect on her.

Betty Nelson, often called the Little Captain, because she was such a born leader, was the only daughter of Mr. and Mrs. Charles Nelson, the former a rich carpet manufacturer. Betty loved, to "do things," as witness her assumption of the summer plans of her chums.

Grace Ford was tall and slender, and often spoken of as a "Gibson" type, by those who admire that artist's peculiar, and always charming, conception of young womanhood. Grace lived with her father and mother, the other member of the family being her brother Will, a hasty, impulsive lad, whose character had, more than once, gotten him into trouble, to the no small annoyance of Grace. Grace had one failing, if such it can be called. She was exceedingly fond of chocolates and other sweets, and was never without some confection in her possession.

And then there was Billy—as Mollie Billette was nicknamed. Mollie was the daughter of a well-to-do widow, Mrs. Pauline Billette, whose French ancestry you could guess by her name and by her appearance and manner. Mollie was a bit French herself. There were two other children, the funny little twins, Paul and "Dodo," as Dora called herself in her lisping fashion. Paul and Dodo were at once the loving care and despair of Mollie and her mother.

So much for the four chums, who were known as the Outdoor Girls.

After their activities, as set down in the first volume of this series, they were next heard of at Rainbow Lake, where, in Betty's motor boat, the Gem, they had some stirring and exciting times.

But, stirring as those times were, they were equalled, if not excelled, when Mollie became possessed of a motor car, and took her chums on a tour which ended only when the mystery of the haunted mansion of Shadow Valley was solved.

Glorious days on skates and iceboats followed, when the outdoor girls went to a winter camp. And then came a contrast when it was learned that Mr. Stonington had purchased an orange grove in Florida, and that Amy had the privilege of inviting her friends to spend the winter in the Sunny South.

For what happened there I refer you to the volume dealing with our friends' activities amid the palms. Sufficient to say that they thoroughly enjoyed themselves. They had returned to Deepdale,

15

their home town on the Argono River, just as spring was budding forth.

And now, this glorious day, the four girls had met once again, and were ready for something new, which something seemed to be offered by Betty Nelson.

"You see it's this way, girls," went on the Little Captain, as she explained matters. "Mother just loves the sea, and she has been wanting a permanent place there for some time. Papa has been looking about, and he heard of Edgemere, a beautiful big cottage, almost on the beach. He said he would buy it if mamma liked it, and so she and I went to look at it to-day."

"You don't mean to say you have been to Ocean View, and back, this same day!" exclaimed Grace, in surprise.

"Yes. We went down on the first train this morning—up before the sun, really, and we arrived before noon. It did not take us long to decide about the cottage. Mamma and I leased it, with the privilege of buying in the fall, if we like it. Then we came back, and on the way, in the train, I asked mamma if I couldn't have you girls down for the summer."

"And she didn't faint at the prospect?" asked Mollie, mischievously.

"The idea!" cried Betty. "Of course not! She was delighted! So, as soon as our train arrived, which was only a few minutes ago, I started looking for you. As I came up from the station, leaving mamma to go home in the car, I spied you three just turning into the candy store."

"Grace is the only one who will 'turn into' a candy store," spoke Mollie. "She will actually turn into a drop of chocolate some day, if she isn't careful."

"Smarty!" mocked the fair one.

"Well, I found you there, at any rate," went on Betty, "and you know the rest; or, rather, you will when I tell you about Edgemere!"

"Edgemere—what's that?" asked Amy.

"It isn't a new kind of confection, even if Grace thinks so," laughed Mollie.

"I—I'll throw something at you if you don't stop!" threatened the Gibson girl, but as all she had in her hand was a chocolate, and as she never would have devoted that to such a purpose, she once more curled up luxuriously on the sofa.

"Edgemere—on the edge of the ocean," translated Betty. "It's the name of our cottage. Now, girls, I'm just dying to have you see it. I brought back some picture postcards of the place. Ocean View is the dearest, quaintest old fishing village you can imagine. It's like Provincetown, somewhat, only different, and——"

"What's that?" suddenly interrupted Grace.

"The boys," spoke Mollie. "As if that awful racket could be anything else."

There sounded on the porch of the Nelson home the heavy tramp of several feet, and the murmur of eager voices.

"Are the girls here?" someone asked.

"That's my brother, Will—bother! I suppose I have to go home," said Grace, petulantly.

"I'll go see," offered Betty. "It sounds like more than Will."

"It is!" cried Mollie, peering under the window shade. "There's Amy's brother, besides Allen Washburn, Roy Anderson and—oh, there's that johnny—Percy Falconer. What in the world can have brought them all here?"

"Natural attractions—the magnet—as the flower draws the bee—and so on and so on," murmured Betty. "I'll ask them in," and she went to meet the boys whose voices could now be heard in the hall.

CHAPTER III

PREPARATIONS

"Hello, Betty!"

"Is Grace here?"

"Where's Amy? I heard she came this way—oh, yes, they're all here, boys. We've found the right place."

"Just in time for five o'clock tea, aren't we!"

"What's that? Did Percy get that off? Just for that he sha'n't have any sweet spirits of nitre!"

A chorus of laughs followed the last remarks, which, in turn, were uttered after the rather drawling manner of a tall, slim, well-dressed lad, whose countenance did not betoken any great amount of intelligence.

"Well, it is *time* for five o'clock tea!" remonstrated the youth who had been characterized by one of the girls as a "johnny" for want of a better term.

"Oh, mercy, girls! Percy's got a wrist watch!" gasped Will Ford in falsetto tones. "The saucy little humming bird! Zip!"

"Behave yourselves or you can't come in!" remonstrated Betty, who had relieved the maid at the door. "What is this, anyhow; a delegation of protest or petition?"

19

"Both," answered Allen Washburn, with a quick, eel-like motion that took him past his chums and placed him at Betty's side. She blushed a little at this act, but did not seem displeased.

"We heard you girls had been seen planning some deep-laid scheme, as you came down the street," went on Will Ford, the brother of Grace, "and we followed. Where is my sainted sister? Making fudge or looking to see if some one is going to treat to sodas?"

"I wouldn't get many sodas if I depended on *you,*" observed Grace, with pointed sarcasm.

"Save me!" ejaculated Will, pretending to hide behind Percy. "Don't let them harm me, will you, old man?"

"Stop!" remonstrated the slim chap, for Will was rather violent in his action, and Percy Falconer was anything but robust. "Besides, you are wrinkling my coat," he added.

"Shades of Beau Brummel!" murmured Roy Anderson, rather tousled in appearance, but with a wholesome, boyish look about him, "Save the wrist watch, Will."

"Say, what's the idea?" asked Mollie, a bit slangily. "Are you going to ask us out? If you are we can't go, for we have important business to transact."

"Yes, fellows, this is the annual session of the Associated Chocolate Fiends," spoke Will. "If you interrupt you'll be fined a box of caramels."

The laughing boys and girls crowded into the library. It was not an unusual occurrence for them all to thus gather at Betty's home, which seemed to be a rendezvous for such little parties. But the boys seldom came in such numbers.

"I wonder why they brought that—Percy," whispered Betty, when she had a chance at Grace's ear.

"No danger—they didn't *bring* him—he *attached* himself," replied Grace. For, be it known, Percy was not very well liked. The boys did not care for him because of his too well-dressed appearance, and his lack of appreciation of manly sports. And the girls did not like him—well, for as much a reason as anything, because Betty did not care for him.

Percy Falconer was, or imagined he was, very fond of Betty. And, to tell more of the truth, Betty distinctly did not care for Percy, though he tried to show her attentions. Now if it had been Allen Washburn, the young law student—well, that is an entirely different story. But as Allen was present on this occasion, the presence of Percy was rather mitigated.

"Girls, we've got news for you!" exclaimed Will, when he and the others had more or less carefully distributed themselves about the library. "Fine and dandy news!"

"The best ever!" added Henry Blackford, with a nod at Amy, who still clung to her modest place behind the palm.

"And, if you're real good, we'll let you in on it," declared Allen Washburn.

"Aren't they condescending, though," mocked Mollie. "As if we didn't have secrets ourselves!"

"Shall we tell them?" asked Grace.

"Let's hear theirs first," suggested Betty.

"What's the matter, Percy, has your wrist watch stopped?" asked Roy Anderson, with a chuckle, for the "johnny" was anxiously holding the timepiece to his ear.

"I—I believe I quite forgot to wind it," was the answer.

"Serious calamity!" murmured Allen, not taking much pains to keep his voice from Percy. That was one thing about the well-dressed youth; he never knew when fun was being poked at him.

"No, it's going all right," Percy spoke, after a silent pause. "It's just five," he added, with a meaning look at Betty.

She choose to ignore it, however, and at a nod from Mollie at once plunged into the matter she and her chums had been discussing when the boys interrupted them.

"We have taken a fine cottage at the shore—Ocean View," said Betty, "and we girls are going to spend the summer there. Don't you boys wish you were us?"

For a moment the young men looked at one another. Then smiles broke over their faces, which were beginning to take on the tan that would be deepened as the summer days approached.

"That sort of takes the edge off our news," spoke Allen. "But we'll tell you, just the same. One of my clients," he began, "has——"

"Hark to him, would you!" broke in Will. "As if he had more than *one* client."

"Oh, Will, can't you be quiet!" rebuked his sister. "Let Allen tell it."

"Yes," urged Roy. "Go on, old man."

"As I was saying, when interrupted by this individual," resumed Allen, "one of my clients, who owns a large motor boat, has decided not to use it this summer. He has offered it to me, and we boys have made up a party to go on a cruise along the New England shore—Martha's Vineyard, Block Island and all that, you know!"

"The New England shore!" cried Betty. "Why, that's where Ocean View is—in New England. If you boys motor along there, can't you come to see us?"

"Of course we can!" exclaimed Allen, quickly. "But we hoped you might be able to take a cruise with us."

"Not a very long one, though we might go for a day or so," went on Betty. "You see, the girls are to be my guests. We were just arranging it when you came in. But we're awfully glad you will be down that way."

"So are we!" exclaimed Roy. "It's a dandy boat Allen has the use of. Sleeping cabin and all that. We can live aboard her. Be out of sight of land for a week, maybe."

"Hardly as long as that," objected Will.

"Why not?" Allen wanted to know.

"I'm expecting news, you know. My appointment—and all that."

"Oh, that's so. I forgot. Well, we could put in every now and then, to see if there was any word for you."

"What's all this?" asked Grace, with a glance at her brother.

"Just a little secret, Sis," he answered.

"Oh, tell me!"

"Not now. Later. Now if you girls———"

"I say!" broke in Percy.

"Hello! He's come to life!" laughed Roy.

"Has your watch stopped again?" demanded Will.

"This is the first I heard about you fellows going on a cruise," went on Percy. "I—I really, I don't know that I can quite make it, don't you know."

"Oh, mercy! What a calamity!" whispered Allen, in the depths of a sofa cushion.

"Will you—will you go out where it is very rough?" asked Percy.

"Rough! You should see the water along the New England coast!" cried Henry Blackford. "Why, even when it's smoothest, a boat nearly turns on her beam ends."

"Would one—er—would one get—er—seasick?" faltered Percy.

"One would—most decidedly!" exclaimed Roy.

"Oh, dear! Then I don't believe I can go," went on the other. "But my father has promised to go for a tour in our motor car, and I may be able to induce him to take in the New England shore. It would be horribly jolly if I could, now; wouldn't it? What? Ha! Ha!" and he beamed on the assembled crowd of young people.

"Most beastly delightful!" mocked Will, in a low voice.

"Where's your place, Betty?" asked Allen.

The Little Captain told him, and the two moved off by themselves for a little chat.

"Say, Will, why don't you want to get too far from shore?" asked Grace of her brother. "What's the secret? I think you might tell me!"

"I will when the time comes," he said, coolly.

"You're not going back to Uncle Isaac's factory; are you?"

"Father Neptune forbid! No."

For, as a punishment for a school scrape, Will had been sent to work in a cotton factory owned by a relative. And, unable to stand the hard conditions there, he had run away, and had had no end of hard times in a turpentine camp, until, on their trip to Florida, the outdoor girls had been instrumental in rescuing him.

"No, I'm not going back there," Will said. "It's a new line of work, Sis, and while I'm waiting for a certain appointment I think I'll go on this cruise with Allen and the others."

"And do you think you'll come to see us at Ocean View?"

"We certainly will!"

A little later the conference of young people broke up. The boys said they must make preparations for their motor boat outing, and naturally Grace, Mollie and Amy were anxious to lay before their folks the invitation from Betty.

"But I'm sure they'll let you come," the latter said. Later that day she received telephone messages from her chums, stating that they could go to the seashore.

"Then get ready as soon as you can!" urged Betty.

"We will," promised Grace. Then as she carried up to her room a box of chocolates she had purchased—the third that day—she murmured to herself: "I wonder what that secret of Will's can be about? I do hope he doesn't get into any more trouble."

CHAPTER IV

OFF FOR OCEAN VIEW

"Are you going to take all those?"

"All those? Why, there aren't so many, Mollie."

"Well, I like your idea of many, Betty. Why, you'll need two trunks for those dresses. Oh, where did you get that pretty linen skirt, and it's quite full, too; isn't it?"

"Yes, they're coming in that way again," and Betty draped the skirt in question over her hip, holding it up for Mollie to see. The two girls were in Betty Nelson's room, and the Little Captain was packing a trunk.

At least that was the official name of the operation. To the uninitiated, or to "mere man," it looked as though nothing was being done except to scatter dresses on chairs, on the bed, divan and other vantage points.

"But I have to lay them all out this way," Betty had explained, when Mollie, running over in an interval of her own packing, to get ready to go to Ocean View, had gasped in wonder at the confusion in her friend's room. "I want to see what I have, so I'll know what to take with me."

"That isn't my way," Mollie laughed. "I simply open a closet door, sweep everything off the hooks and toss them into a trunk. Then I get Felice to jump on the lid with me, and—presto! the trick is done, Madame!" and she laughed and shrugged her shoulders in pretty little French fashion.

"I simply can't do it that way," sighed Betty. "I suppose it does take a long time to lay each dress out separately, but——"

"It is much more kind to the dresses," agreed Mollie. "That's why you always look so nice, and why I always appear so—so——"

"Don't you dare say a word about yourself, Mollie Billette!" protested Betty. "You always look so sweet. Why, you can take an old piece of cloth and a couple of faded flowers, and make of it a hat that looks prettier than one mamma pays Madame Rosenti twelve dollars for when I go with her. I don't see how you manage to do it."

"It was born in me!" laughed the French girl, as with a quick motion she draped one of Betty's garments about her shoulders, producing an effect at which Betty gasped in pleasure.

"Now, why doesn't that ever look like that on me?" she demanded.

"Betty, you're a dear!" replied Mollie, without answering. "Now I am keeping you. I must run back. I haven't begun to pack yet, and I know Paul and Dodo will have my room in dreadful shape. They are probably, at this minute, parading around in my best frocks, playing soldier," and Mollie with a laughing kiss for her chum jumped up and fled from the room to hurry home and minimize the work of the playful twins.

"Don't forget the time!" cried Betty, after her chum, leaning out of the window of her room, and breathing in deep of the balmy June air. "We leave a week from to-day."

"Oh, I won't forget!" answered Mollie. "It is altogether too delightful for that."

Betty resumed her inspection of dresses, to determine which she should take, while Mollie hastened home. But Betty had not long been alone when the doorbell tinkled and Grace Ford was announced.

"Tell her to come right up, if she will," Betty directed the maid, and the tall, willowy one entered with a rush and a rustling of silken skirts.

"My!" gasped Betty, looking up from her position, kneeling amid a pile of clothes. "All dressed up and no place to go, Grace! What does it mean? No, thank you, no chocolates when I'm looking over my pretty things. I might spot them."

"That's just what happened to me," sighed the Gibson girl. "I had to put on my best silk petticoat, as I spilled a lot of chocolate down my other. I sent it away to be cleaned, and that's why I'm wearing my best one. Don't you just love the swish of silk?"

"I guess we all do," answered Betty. "Oh, dear!"

"What's the matter?" asked Grace. "Oh, but you are going at it wholesale; aren't you?" as she surveyed the room overflowing with clothes.

"Have to, my dear. It means an all-summer stay, you know. And I don't know what to take and what to leave. I'm sure to want the very things I don't take."

"Take them all, then. That's what I'm doing. Only I haven't really begun yet. I just ran over to ask you something."

"Well, let it be something very easy, Grace dear. My brain isn't capable of taking in very much this morning."

"It's about Will," went on Grace, thoughtfully selecting a chocolate from a bag. "Are you sure you won't have some?" she asked.

"What, of Will? No, thank you!"

"Silly, of course not. I mean this candy. It's delicious! Just fresh and——"

"Cloying," interrupted Betty. "You haven't a lime drop, have you?"

"Ugh! The horrid, sour things, no! But about Will. Did you know he had a secret Betty?"

"A secret? Mercy, no! Is it about some——"

"I don't believe it's a girl. If it is, Will acts the funniest of anyone I ever saw. He has a lot of books and papers he's studying over."

"It might be her—letters—or—her picture that he puts in a book so no one will see——"

"It isn't that!" declared Grace with conviction. "Oh, this is a nougat!" she exclaimed in rapture, as her white teeth bit into a particularly delicious candy.

"Hopeless!" sighed Betty, folding a skirt neatly.

"I mean he hasn't any girl's picture, or anything like that," went on Grace. "I found one of the books where he had laid it down. It is some sort of Government report. I thought you might know.

"Why?" asked Betty, quickly. "I'm not in his confidence."

"I know, but you see, Will and Allen being so chummy, and Allen being so fond of you——"

"Grace Ford!" broke in Betty. "You shouldn't say such things!" and she blushed crimson.

"Why not?" demanded Grace, coolly. "There's no one here but us, and we know it. I thought perhaps Will had told Allen, and Allen might have hinted to you."

"Not a word, Grace, dear. I didn't even know Will had a secret."

"Well, he has, and he won't tell me. But I'll find out. He's up to something. I only hope he doesn't run away again, or do something foolish."

"Will doesn't mean anything," declared Betty. "He is just high-spirited; that's all. What sort of a secret did it seem to be, if it wasn't about—girls?" and Betty laughed.

"Oh, I'm sure it isn't about girls," Grace went on, seriously enough. "At least it isn't any girl in our set, and Will doesn't know any others. And if it is some one in our set, they're all nice girls, so it won't really matter—after we get used to it."

"Oh, dear!" laughed Betty. "You speak as though he were engaged!"

"Oh, I know he isn't," declared Grace. "But he is such a tease. But if you don't know, you don't, Betty. And now I must run back. Have any of the other members of the club been over?"

"Yes, Mollie was just here."

Grace fished out another chocolate, after shaking up the bag to see if there were any choice ones at the bottom, and then, after trying in vain to induce Betty to accept a sweet, took her departure, saying she was going to see to her own packing.

"Now it only needs a call from Amy to make the round of visits complete," murmured Betty, as she resumed the sorting of her garments. But Amy did not come that morning.

The outdoor girls were making ready for their trip to Ocean View, where the better part of the summer would be spent.

The arrangements had been made for the Nelson family to occupy the beautiful cottage, Edgemere, which was completely furnished.

"Even to matches and a candle in each bedroom," Betty had said.

"But I thought you said it was a modern place," objected Grace. "I don't like candles—excuse me, Betty dear, but they are so—so smelly!"

"I know. The candles are only for emergency. The house has electric lights."

"Electric lights! I thought Ocean View was such a *quaint* old place," murmured Mollie.

"So it is. The electric plant is in Point Lomar, that swell summer resort. Only a few places in Ocean View have electricity."

And so the arrangements went on. Mollie, Grace and Amy were to be Betty's guests during the summer, though their parents or relatives had a standing invitation to spend week-ends and holidays at the shore.

"And of course the boys are always welcome!" added Betty.

"And of course we'll come!" declared Will and the others. "That is, I'll spend as much time as I can away from my official duties!"

"Oh, he nearly told us then!" cried Grace. "Will, I'll never speak to you again, if you don't tell me that secret."

"You shall know in due time, sister mine. As for your threat, I don't mind your not speaking to me if you don't make me buy your chocolates. I care not who speaks to me!" he paraphrased, "as long as I do not have to buy their candy!"

"Here comes Percy Falconer!" interrupted Roy, and the little conference, one of many held whenever the friends met—broke up.

While the girls were getting ready with trunks of clothes, the boys were no less busily engaged. They had completed their plans for a series of cruises along the coast, in the motor boat *Pocohontas*, loaned to Allen Washburn by a wealthy gentleman for whom he had done some law business, though Allen was not as yet admitted to the bar.

"I'll have a chance to practice this summer, getting the boat off a sand-bar!" he had jokingly said.

And finally trunks were packed, tickets had been purchased, word had come from Ocean View that the cottage was in readiness, and at last, on a beautifully sunny June morning, the outdoor girls stood at the station, ready to take the train.

The boys were there, also, as might have been guessed.

"And when are you coming down in the boat?" asked Betty.

"In about a week," Allen said. "We're having the engine overhauled, a new magneto put in and some other things done."

"I'm coming in the auto," broke in Percy Falconer. "Father did not want me to make the boat trip, but the chauffeur will bring me down to the shore in the car."

"Pity he wouldn't use a feather bed," murmured Roy Anderson.

"Oh, here comes the train!" cried Mollie. "Girls, I'm almost sure I've forgotten half my things."

"Good-bye, girls!" chorused the boys.

"Good-bye!" came the answer.

"Oh, Grace!" called Will to his sister.

"Yes," she answered.

"That secret of mine."

"Oh, yes. What is it? Do tell me! I haven't a second——"

"I'll tell you—when I come down!" his words floated to her as she was borne along the platform with her chums to the train that was to take them to Ocean View.

CHAPTER V

OLD TIN-BACK

"Isn't he provoking!" murmured Grace, sinking into a seat beside Mollie, as the train slowly pulled out.

"Who?" asked Mollie, leaning toward the window to wave to the boys on the platform.

"My brother Will. He's up to something—he has a secret and he won't tell me!"

"Don't let him know you care, and he'll tell you all the quicker. Boys are that way," declared Mollie, with the accumulated wisdom of—say—seventeen years.

"Yes, I suppose so," agreed Grace, and then she began a hurried search among the various articles she had deposited on the seat between herself and Mollie.

"What is it—lost something?" asked the latter.

"My bag of—oh, here they are," and Grace, with a look of contentment, began munching some chocolates.

"It is awfully nice of you, Mrs. Nelson, to ask us down for the summer," said Amy Blackford to her hostess when they were settled in the speeding train. "I do so love the seashore."

"Then I think you will like it at Ocean View," remarked Betty's mother. "And we think Edgemere a pretty place."

"I'm sure it must be from what Betty has told me."

"Do you like lobsters?" asked Mr. Nelson, looking over the top of his paper, with a twinkle in his eyes.

"Lobsters?" repeated Amy, questioningly. "I haven't eaten many."

"It's a great place for lobsters at Ocean View," went on Betty's father. "That's one reason I decided on it."

"The idea!" cried his wife. "To hear you talk anyone would think you never ate anything else, and you know if you take too much *a la Newburg* you don't feel well the next day."

"I'm going to take only the plain boiled, and salads," declared Mr. Nelson. "But there's an old lobsterman—Tin-Back, they call him—near Edgemere in whom I think you girls will be interested," he went on. "He's quite a character.

"Why do they call him Tin-Back?" asked Amy. "Has he really a——"

"A tin back? How funny that would be?" laughed Betty.

"You must ask him," declared her father. "I didn't have time when I came down to see if everything was all right."

"Oh, what lovely times we'll have, girls!" sighed Mollie, when, a little later, the four chums were conversing. "We can go sailing, bathing and sit on the sands and watch the tide come in."

"And perhaps find buried pirate-treasure in some cave," added Betty, with a laugh.

"Can we, really?" asked Amy, perhaps the most unsophisticated of the quartette.

"Really what?" asked Grace, silently offering her bag of sweets. The habit was almost automatic with her.

"Find buried treasure," said Amy, eagerly. "I should love to do that. I've often read——"

"That's all you can do—read about it," spoke Mollie, regretfully. "There isn't any romance left in this world. If there was a pirate's cave it would be lighted with electricity and an admission fee charged. And yet the New England coast ought to contain some treasure. Some pirates used to land there."

"Did they, Mr. Nelson?" asked Amy, catching sight of Betty's father again glancing over the top of his paper.

"Did pirates ever land on the coast near where we are going?"

"Well, perhaps, yes. I believe there are several stories about Kidd's treasure being buried somewhere around Ocean View. Or, perhaps it would be more correct to say that one of Kidd's treasures. On the very lowest count he must have had at least a double score, all hidden in different places."

"Really?" demanded Amy, with glistening eyes, and flushed cheeks.

"Well, as really as any other treasure story, I suppose," answered Mr. Nelson, while Betty murmured:

"Oh, Daddy! Don't tease her!"

"I'm not!" he declared. "It is possible that there may be some treasure buried in the sand near Ocean View. Stranger things have happened."

"Oh, what if we should find it!" cried Amy. "I'm going to look the first thing I do."

"Find what?" asked Grace, who had been looking from the window as they passed through a town.

"Buried treasure," Amy said.

"Oh, I thought you meant Will's secret," observed Grace. "I wonder where that train boy is?" she went on.

"What for?" asked Betty.

"I want another box of those chocolates. They were a new kind and——"

"Grace Ford! If you buy another bit of candy before we arrive I——I don't know what I'll do to you!" threatened Betty.

The train rolled on, as all trains do, and, eventually, the little seaside resort of Ocean View was reached. There was the usual scramble on the part of our friends, and other passengers, to alight, and when the girls stood on the rather dingy platform of the station Mollie, looking about her in some disappointment, said:

"Ocean View! I don't see why they call it that. You can't see the ocean at all."

"It's down that way," said Mr. Nelson, with a wave of his hand toward the east. "Property is too valuable along the shore to allow of the village being there. The town is about a mile back from the water. We'll take a carriage to the cottage. You see the railroad doesn't run very close to the ocean."

Ocean View was like most summer resorts, built some distance back from the shore, which property was held by cottage or bungalow owners. There were several shell roads running from the main street of the town down to the water's edge, however. And soon, in a carriage, with their valises piled around them, our party set off for Edgemere, leaving a truckman to bring the trunks.

"Oh what a perfectly dear place!" exclaimed Grace, as the carriage turned along a highway that paralleled the beach. "And how blue the water is!"

They were up on a little elevation. Down below them was a large bay, enclosed in a point of land that ran out into the ocean, forming a perfect breakwater.

"Where is Edgemere?" asked Mollie.

"Over there," answered Betty, pointing.

The girls beheld a large cottage nestling amid a group of evergreen and other trees, on the very point of land that jutted out, with the bay on one side and the ocean on the other.

"Oh, how perfectly charming!" exclaimed Amy. "And we can have still water bathing as well as that in the surf."

"Exactly," answered Betty. "That's why mamma and I decided on it. I like still water myself."

"So do I," murmured Amy.

"I don't! I want the boiling surf!" declared Mollie, who was an excellent swimmer.

They drove up to the cottage, finding new delights every moment, and when the carriage stopped within the fence, at the side porch, the whole party waited a moment before alighting to admire the place.

"It is nice," decided Mrs. Nelson. "I had forgotten part of it, but I like it even better than I thought I should."

"It's sweet!" declared Grace.

"Horribly fascinating, as Percy Falconer would say," mocked Mollie.

"Don't!" begged Betty, making a wry face.

As they were alighting, a quaint figure of an old man, bent and shuffling, with gnarled and twisted hands, and a face almost lost in a bush of beard, yet in whose blue eyes twinkled kindliness and good fellowship, came around the side path.

"Wa'al, I see ye got here!" he exclaimed in hoarse tones—his voice seemed to be coming out of a perpetual fog.

"Yes, we've arrived," Mr. Nelson said.

"Glad ye come. Ye'll find everything all ready for ye! 'Mandy has a fire goin', an th' chowder's hot."

"Who is he?" asked Mrs. Nelson, in a whisper.

"Old Tin-Back," replied her husband. "He's a lobsterman and a character. I engaged his wife to clean the cottage, and be here when you arrived."

"Yes, I'm Old Tin-Back," replied the man with a gruff but not unpleasant laugh. "Leastways they all calls me that. I'll take them grips," he went on, as the girls advanced, and into his gnarled hands he gathered the valises.

"Oh, what a delicious smell!" exclaimed Mollie, as they went up the steps.

"That's th' chowder," chuckled the old lobsterman. "I reckoned it'd be tasty. Plenty of quahogs in *that*."

"What?" gasped Amy.

"Quahogs—big clams, miss," he explained. "Old Tin-Back dug 'em this mornin' at low tide. Nothin' like quahogs for chowder, though some folks likes soft clams. But not for Old Tin-Back."

"Is—is that really your name?" asked Amy.

"Wa'al not *really*, miss. It's a sort of nickname. You see, I sell clams, lobsters and crabs, but I don't never sell no tin-back crabs, and so they sorter got in the habit of callin' me that."

"What are tin-backs?" asked Amy, but before the lobsterman could answer, Betty, from within the cottage, called to her chums:

"Come, girls, and select your rooms!"

CHAPTER VI

THE BOYS

Amy remained standing beside the old lobsterman. Mollie and Grace had followed Mrs. Nelson and Betty into the cottage. Mr. Nelson was paying the carriage driver, and arranging to have some things brought over from the station.

"Tin-backs," repeated Amy. "What sort of crabs are they?"

"Soft crabs, just turnin' hard, miss," explained the old man. "If you punch in their backs they spring up and down like the bottom of a tin dish pan. That's why they call 'em that. Tin-backs is tough to eat. I never sell 'em, though some folks do. That's why they call me that, I guess."

"Oh!" remarked Amy. "Then that means you are—honest!"

"Wa'al, miss, I don't lay no special claims to virtue," he protested.

"But if you don't sell tinny crabs—ugh, how funny that sounds—then you *must* be honest!" Amy insisted. "I'm so glad to know you. Tell me, is there any pirate's treasure buried around here?"

Old Tin-Back looked at her, startled. Then he edged away slightly.

"Exactly," laughingly said Amy afterward, "as though I had announced that I was a militant suffragist, and intended burning his boats."

"Pirate's treasure, miss?" repeated the old lobsterman. "I—er—I never found any."

"But Mr. Nelson said there might be some."

"Oh, there *might*—yes. And I *might* find a dead whale with a lump of ambergris in him, as big as a barrel," spoke Tin-Back, "but I never *have*."

"What's ambergris?" asked Amy, who rather enjoyed his talk.

"I don't rightly know, miss, but it's something like a lump of suet in a dead whale, and it's worth its weight in gold. It makes perfume!"

"The idea," murmured Amy, with a little shudder. "I don't believe I shall like perfume after that."

"Oh, I don't s'pose they use none of it around Ocean View," spoke Old Tin-Back, with a frank air. "Anyhow, we never see a dead whale in these parts. There was one once, but folks was glad when the high tide carried him out to sea. I guess they're callin' you," he added.

Amy was aware of Betty summoning her within the cottage. She smiled at Tin-Back and entered the house.

"Where were you?" demanded Betty. "I want you to see which room you like best. There are several to choose from."

"I was talking with the lobsterman," explained Amy. "He is called Tin-Back because he never sells that sort of crab, and he hopes he can find a lump of ambergris in a dead whale some day."

"Well, if that isn't a combination!" laughed Mollie. "Oh, but I think my room is the *dearest* one! Come and see it, Amy."

"Not until she selects her own," decided Betty.

Then began the settling down in the charming cottage of Edgemere at Ocean View. The girls had bedrooms adjoining, and across from one another along a hall that ran the whole length of the house, and ended in a little open balcony at either end. The house stood on a point of land, and from one end a view could be had of the ocean, while the other opened on Lobster Bay. There was a large plot of ground around the Nelson cottage so that other bungalows were not too near. And it was in the midst of a little summer colony of houses, so, though it stood rather by itself, the place was not in the least lonesome.

Trunks were unpacked, valises stripped of their contents, closets and chiffoniers filled, bureaus blossomed with a wonderful collection of combs, brushes, barettes, ribbons, and various bottles and jars. For, though the outdoor girls were not afraid of sun, wind or rain, Betty had warned them that sunburn was not an ailment to be rashly courted, and that cold cream, or talcum powder, judiciously used, might lessen many a smart.

Behold our friends then, a little later, well fortified within with clam chowder and other dainties prepared by 'Mandy, the wife of Old Tin-Back, strolling along the ocean beach. Mrs. Nelson was superintending the efforts of the maid to bring some order out of chaos at the cottage.

"It is perfectly lovely!" murmured Mollie, as she and her chums walked along the strand. "Charming."

"And so sweet of you to ask us down, Betty dear!" declared Grace.

"Oh, it was partly selfishness," Betty admitted. "I didn't want to stay here all summer alone."

"May we always meet with that sort of selfishness," observed Amy.

"I wonder when the boys will come," went on Grace.

"Lonesome already?" asked Betty, smiling.

"No. But Will promised to let me know what new plans he had when he came, and I've tried so hard to guess his secret that I'm tired."

"Give it up," advised Mollie. "Oh, look what pretty shells!" and she gathered several from the sand.

"How damp it is!" exclaimed Grace. "Positively, there isn't a bit of curl left in my hair. But just look at Amy's! I never saw it so pretty!"

"The salt air agrees with hers," said Betty. "We'll all have nice complexions if this Newport fog continues," and she indicated the mist arising from the sea.

"Let's sit down and just look at the ocean," suggested Amy, when they had walked some distance down the beach, and while they were thus idly employed, and when the afternoon was waning, they spied a solitary figure approaching them down the stretch of sand.

"It's Old Tin-Back," said Betty. "I wonder if he is looking for us?"

"He seems to be looking for something on the beach," commented Grace, "and unless he thinks we have slipped down one of those funny little holes the sand fleas make, I can't see how he could be searching for us."

But the old lobsterman had a message for them, nevertheless, for when he came within hailing distance he called hoarsely:

"Ahoy there, young ladies! Your folks want you to come back. I told 'em I'd tell you if I saw you as I come along, and I done it."

"What were you looking for—treasure?" asked Grace, with a mischievous smile at Amy.

"Treasure? Humph, no, miss. I was looking for some of my lobster pots. A lot of them dragged their moorings in the last storm, and they get cast upon the beach sooner or later."

"Did you ever find any treasure on the beach?" demanded Betty.

"Wa'al, no, not exactly what you could call *treasure!*" was the slow and cautious answer, "but I did find a pipe once, an' it lasted me for quite a while. Found it jest after I lost my corncob, too. So, in a manner of speakin', I did find suthin'."

"But never gold, or diamonds or *real* treasure, washed up from a wreck?" asked Amy, eagerly.

"No, miss."

"Are there ever wrecks?" inquired Betty.

"Oh, yes, once in a while, though not usually this time of year. In the winter the sea's altogether different, miss. It's terrible cruel and cold. Then we have wrecks. Why, right off there, two year ago," and with a gnarled finger he pointed though at no particular object as far as the girls could see, "right off there a three-master went down one night in a January, and all hands—eleven of 'em—was drowned."

"Didn't anyone try to save them?" asked Grace.

THE OLD LOBSTERMAN PEERED THROUGH A BATTERED
SPY-GLASS. "THAT'S HER," HE ANNOUNCED.—Page 51.

The Outdoor Girls at Ocean View.

"Oh, yes, they tried, miss, but they couldn't launch the boat, and the wind was blowin' so they couldn't shoot a line over. The boat went to pieces on the bar, and the bodies washed ashore next day."

He told it simply, and was silent for a space.

"Does anything ever wash ashore from the wrecks?" asked Mollie.

"Oh, yes, once in a while, but not what you could rightly call treasure. Once a banana steamer got on the bar, and they had to throw over lots of cargo to lighten her. Folks here made quite a tidy sum collectin' them bunches of green bananas."

"But no boxes of gold or diamonds—mysterious, locked boxes?" asked Amy, still hopefully.

"No, miss, nothin' like that," and Old Tin-Back looked as though he was not altogether sure whether or not he was being made fun of.

The days passed at Ocean View, sunny, happy days. Each one brought new pleasure and delight to the outdoor girls, and they lived up to their name, for they were seldom in the house. They bathed and rowed in the bay, or paid visits to the quaint little town, where Grace discovered an old French woman who made delicious taffy.

"So Grace's happiness is assured for the summer," declared Mollie.

Then came a day when, as the four went down to see Old Tin-Back set off from the little dock in his dory to take up his lobster pots, they saw a motor boat heading into the bay.

51

"Oh, if that should be the boys!" exclaimed Grace, hopefully. "They wrote they might come this week; didn't they?"

"Yes," answered Betty.

"What boat ye lookin' fer?" asked Tin-Back.

"The *Pocohontas*," answered Amy.

The old lobsterman peered through a battered spyglass he took from a locker-box in his dory.

"That's her," he announced.

And so it proved. The big motor boat swung up to the dock and Will, Roy, Henry and Allen smiled at the girls.

"Well, we're here, you see!" announced Grace's brother. "This is the first real stop of our cruise. Been having a fine time these last five days. But we're glad we're here."

"And we're glad to see you!" responded Betty. "Do come up to the cottage. Mamma will want to see you. How long can you stay?"

"Oh, a week—two weeks—a month in a place like this with—ahem! such nice girls!" remarked Roy.

"Oh, what's that? You scratched me!" exclaimed Grace as she suffered her brother to imprint a sort of half-way kiss on her cheek. His coat blew open, disclosing something shining through an armhole of his vest.

"Oh, that's my—badge!" he announced.

"Your badge? What are you, a pilot?" demanded Amy.

"Ahem! At your service!" exclaimed Will, with a low bow, as he extended a card to his sister. Grace fairly grabbed it from him, and read her brother's name, while, in a corner of the pasteboard, under a monogram device, were the letters "U. S. S. S."

"What does it mean?" she asked.

"That's the secret," Will explained. "I have joined the United States Secret Service, sister mine!"

"Secret Service!" repeated Grace. "What does it mean?"

"It means I'm out for smugglers, counterlaws. So beware!"

CHAPTER VII

THE STORM

For a moment or two the girls did not know whether or not to accept as truth the statement Will had made in such a dramatic manner. Then his sister Grace burst out with:

"Oh, Will, is it really true? Is that the secret you were going to tell me?"

"That's the secret, Sis! Isn't it a good one, and didn't I keep it well?"

"You certainly did, but I didn't expect it would be that. I thought it would be about—about—er——"

She paused in some confusion.

"She thought it would be about a *girl!*" broke in Mollie. "Why wasn't it, Will?"

"It may be yet. There are lady smugglers, you know!"

"Oh, nonsense!"

"Will Ford!"

"Is it really true?"

"I think he's just teasing us!"

Thus cried the girls in turn, Betty appealing to Allen in an aside to know whether Will really had been appointed to a government position.

"Oh, yes, its true enough," Allen said, smiling indulgently.

And finally, after a little gale of laughter had subsided, Will managed to make the girls, his sister included, understand, and believe that he really was telling the truth. Then they inspected his badge, looked at a sort of identifying card he carried in an inner pocket, and were satisfied.

"But what does it all mean?" asked Grace. "I didn't know you were going in for that sort of thing, Will! How did it happen? And are there any smugglers around here?"

"Hist! Not a word! Sush! Take care!" hissed her brother, stepping about with elaborate precautions on tiptoes, glancing rapidly from side to side, while he flashed a pretended dark lantern, and Allen imitated the low, shivery music of a Chinese orchestra.

"They may be here any minute!" chanted Will in dramatic tones. "Quick! We must hide those diamonds. And then, gal, at the peril of your life, you must give me those papers!" and he hissed after the manner of some stage villains.

"Oh, quit your fooling and tell us!" demanded Grace. "Then we'll go for a ride in your boat, and you can stop at the Point and get me some chocolates, Will."

"Oh, I can, eh? Awfully kind, I'm sure."

"Do tell us about it," begged Amy.

"Ah, at least *you* are sincere!" exclaimed Will, with a look that made gentle Amy blush.

"Go on," urged Roy. "Then we'll get out on the water again. This weather is too good to miss."

"It was this way," explained Will. "I told dad I wanted a little longer vacation before I started in for college, after my experiences in that turpentine camp, and he agreed that I could have it. I don't know whether I told you or not, but when I ran away from Uncle Isaac's down South, I fell in with a Government Secret Service man. I guess he rather suspected I was up to some game, but he was real decent about it, and didn't give me away.

"I happened to do him a favor—helped him trail a certain man he was looking for, and he was good enough to compliment me on my memory for faces. He said it was the beginning of a successful detective's career.

"Well, I had no notion of being a detective, but it made me stop and think. I am pretty good at remembering faces and voices, you know, even if I do say it myself."

"That's right!" chimed in Allen. "I wish I had that faculty. It is the hardest thing for me to remember the faces and names of those I meet. But go on, Will."

"Well, the upshot of it was that this government man said if I ever wanted a lift he'd be glad to help me. He gave me his card, and, after all my troubles were over, thanks to your efforts, girls," and he included them all in his bow, "I decided to go in for Secret Service work.

"It wasn't as easy as I had expected, but at last I got the promise of a chance, and I began studying up, and taking the examinations. I passed successfully, and received my commission."

"So that's what you were doing all those days you were away so much?" asked Grace.

"That was it, Sis. And now I am a full fledged Secret Service agent, though I haven't arrested anyone yet."

"And are you really going to?" asked Betty.

"That all depends," replied Will. "If I see any law violations I'll have to."

"But are you looking for anyone in particular, up here?" asked Amy. "Any smugglers, pirates, or—or anything like that?"

"Bless her heart! She shall see a pirate arrested the first chance I have!" laughed Will.

"Oh, be serious, can't you?" asked Grace, with just the hint of a snap in her voice.

"Beg your pardon, Amy," apologized Will. "You see it's this way. I'm in the Boston district, and that takes in a good part of the New England coast. I haven't really been assigned to any particular locality yet. I'm supposed to keep my eyes open wherever I am, though."

"Around here?" Mollie wanted to know.

"Yes, here as well as anywhere else. But I'm on a leave of absence now. I'm spending a few days cruising with the boys. I'll soon have to go back to Boston."

"Well, then busy yourself and buy me those chocolates!" demanded Grace. "You don't need to act in your official capacity for that."

"Do you really think there may be pirates or smugglers around here?" asked Amy, who seemed strangely interested in the matter.

"Well, there might be. You never can tell," said Will, with a look around the horizon as though to discover some mysterious and suspicious vessel in the offing.

After Will's explanations he had to answer a hail of questions from the girls. The boys already knew all he could tell them. Then his sister and her chums wished him all kinds of good luck.

"And I hope we see you arrest your first smuggler!" exclaimed Mollie, with a quick gesture of her expressive hands and shoulders.

"Oh, I don't!" cried Amy, with a nervous look behind her.

"Well, if we're going to take the girls for a ride let's do it," suggested Allen.

"How does the boat run?" asked Betty, as she turned her attention to it.

"Fine and dandy!" he exclaimed with enthusiasm.

A little later the merry party of young people were out on the wide, blue waters of the bay.

Several gladsome days followed. The boys were welcomed at Edgemere, and, as the cottage was a large one, Mrs. Nelson insisted on Will and his chums remaining there, though they said they wanted to camp out, or sleep aboard the *Pocohontas*. But the quarters there were rather cramped.

One day, when the boys were coming back in the boat with the girls, the engine suddenly stopped while they were still a short distance from the dock.

"Hello! What's up? Trouble?" asked Roy.

"Yes, it's that magneto again," decided Allen. "I think I'd better tie her up and get a new one. It will be giving us trouble all summer if I don't."

And then, as the craft was ingloriously paddled up to the dock, the boys held a mysterious conversation regarding ground-wires, brushes, platinum points, spark plugs and batteries.

"Oh, will the boat have to go to the repair shop?" asked Betty.

"Will you be sorry?" returned Allen, meaningly.

"You know I shall. I do so enjoy—the water," she answered with a little blush and a bright glance.

"You sha'n't miss anything," he declared. "I'll charter a sailboat while the *Pocohontas* is laid up."

And this he did, arranging with Old Tin-Back for the hire of a catboat that would hold all the party. Thus the glorious summer days were used to best advantage, the young people cruising about the bay, fishing and bathing as suited their fancy.

"Not going out to-day; are ye?" asked Old Tin-Back, as he came down to the dock one morning, and found the boys and girls about to start off.

"We certainly are!" declared Will. "I think something will happen to-day. I have a feeling in my bones that I may land a smuggler or two."

"Oh, Will!" expostulated his sister. "Don't joke. That may be serious."

"I only hope it *is* serious," he declared.

"What's the matter with going out to-day?" asked Allen.

"Wa'al, it looks like a squall," replied the old lobsterman. "If ye do go don't go out too far."

"Oh, I don't want to go!" objected Grace.

The others laughed Grace out of her fears, and they started off in the sailboat, the motor craft having been left at the repair dock some distance up the coast.

As they swung and dipped over the blue waters of the bay, the signs of the storm increased, and the girls, becoming more and more nervous, insisted on the boys keeping close to shore.

And finally, when they were some distance from Ocean View, but fortunately near a little sheltering cove, the storm broke with sudden fury.

"Down with that sail!" yelled Allen, as the gust struck the boat, heeling her over so that one rail dipped well under water.

"Oh, we're going to capsize!" screamed Grace.

"Keep still!" ordered her brother.

With frightened eyes the girls clung to one another, huddled together in the little cockpit cabin, while a big wave coming from the stern seemed to threaten to swamp them.

CHAPTER VIII

THE MEN IN THE BOAT

"Oh! Oh!" screamed Grace. "We'll be drowned!"

"Nonsense! Keep quiet!" commanded Will, with the authority only a brother could have displayed on such an occasion. His stern voice had the desired effect and Grace ceased clinging to her chums with a grip that really endangered them.

"Oh, I'm so sorry I was silly!" she exclaimed contritely, as the big wave passed harmlessly under the sailboat. Then the craft swung behind a projecting point of land and they were in calmer waters. Allen had let the sail come down on the run, and all danger of capsizing was over. The wind still blew in fitful gusts, however, and the rain, which had been holding off, came down in a drenching shower.

"Get out the mackintoshes!" cried Roy, for those garments had been brought with them at the suggestion of Old Tin-Back.

Protected now against the downpour, and in calmer waters, the young people were themselves once more. The jib gave way enough to the craft for Allen to head it toward a little dock which seemed to be the landing place of the neighborhood fishermen.

"What are you going to do?" asked Will. "Stay here until the storm is over?"

"Might as well," Allen answered. "And yet—hello! What's that?" he interrupted himself suddenly, pointing out to the bay.

"A motor boat broken loose from its mooring," answered Roy.

"And if it isn't the *Pocohontas* I miss my guess!" added Amy's brother.

"That's right!" declared Allen. "John's repair shop is in this cove. He must have anchored her out, and the storm tore her loose. He evidently doesn't know it."

"Well, we know it!" cried Will, "and she'll be on those rocks in a few minutes more. See! She's drifting right toward them!"

It needed but a glance to disclose this. The drifting motor boat, under the influence of wind and waves, was heading straight toward some half-submerged but sharp rocks that were a danger-point in the little cove.

"What's to be done?" demanded Roy.

"You must save your boat, that's certain!" put in Betty, thus sustaining her reputation as a Little Captain.

"We've got to," said Will. "But to take you girls out there again——"

"Don't you dare do it, in this storm!" broke in Grace, for the wind and rain had now reached their height.

"Can't you land us?" asked Betty, taking in the situation at a glance. "That will be best. Put us on shore and then this boat will be so much easier to handle. The wind is right, and you can get the *Pocohontas* before she goes on the rocks."

"She's got the idea," declared Allen, admiringly. "We can save our boat, if we hustle."

"Then—'hustle'!" cried Betty, with a little blush, as she shook her head to rid her flashing eyes of raindrops. "Put us ashore at the dock, and save the *Pocohontas*."

"But what will you do?" asked Allen. "I don't like to leave you on the beach alone."

"We four girls won't be lonesome," declared Mollie. "It isn't the first time we've roughed it. Besides, there is some sort of a fisherman's shanty there. We'll go inside, if the storm gets too bad. But I think it is going to clear."

Indeed there were indications that the weather at least was going to get no worse. There was a hasty conference among the boys, who cast anxious eyes toward their drifting boat. Then the sailing craft was worked up to the little dock, and the girls sprang out.

"We'll come back for you," promised Will.

"If you can't it will be all right," Betty assured him. "We can walk back along the beach after the storm. It isn't more than a mile or two, and we haven't done very much walking lately."

"Well, we'll see what happens," spoke Allen, anxious to get out to the *Pocohontas*, which was dangerously near the rocks.

The girls paused on the dock a moment, to watch the boys beating back out over the bay, and then turned to go up the beach. They had never been on this part of the coast before. It was lonesome and deserted, save for one rather shabby hut just above high-water mark. Over beyond some distant sand dunes, the boys had been told, was the establishment of the boat-builder, where they had taken their craft to have a new magneto put in.

"Shall we go in and ask for shelter?" asked Amy, as they neared the hut.

"Well, it's raining pretty hard," returned Grace.

"Oh, don't let's go in!" said Betty, suddenly, as she looked at a window of the hut. "It's much nicer outside."

"But it's raining so!" protested Mollie, with a quick look at her chum.

"I know. But we're neither sugar nor salt, and this isn't the first rain we've been out in. Besides, I'm sure, in there, it will smell of—fish! I can't bear to be shut up in a stuffy cabin that smells of fish. I vote we stay out. See, it is beginning to clear already," and she pointed to a streak of light in the west.

"Is that your real reason—a dislike of the smell of—fish?" asked Mollie, in a low voice, that Betty alone could hear.

"Not exactly, no," was the reply, equally guarded. "I happened to catch a glimpse of some faces at the window of that hut, and I did not like the look of them—they were—ugh! I don't know what to say," and Betty gave a slight shiver that was not caused entirely by the chilling rain.

"I saw them, too," spoke Mollie, in louder tones now, for Grace and Amy had walked on ahead. "And one of them was—a woman's face."

"Yes, but such a face!" agreed Betty. "It was hard—cruel—oh, I'll never go in that hut."

"Nor will I. The rain is stopping, I think."

"Then let's walk back to Ocean View," proposed Betty. "What do you say, girls?" she called to Amy and Grace. "Shall we walk back? It's stopping, and the sand will be firm and hard after the rain."

"I don't mind," spoke Amy, always willing to be accommodating.

"Oh, well, I suppose we'll have to, if the boys don't come for us," assented Grace.

"They won't be back for some time," declared Betty. "See, they have just reached the boat, and in time, too, I think. A little later she would have been on the rocks."

Allen and his chums had indeed been fortunate in saving the *Pocohontas*. Through the clearing air the girls watched them preparing to tow the motor craft back.

"It will be some time before they can come for us," repeated Betty. "We might as well go on."

"But they won't know where we are," objected Grace, who did not altogether relish the idea of walking. She was wearing shoes with very high heels.

"They'll understand," responded Betty. "See, they are looking this way. I'll give them some sign language they'll understand," and she began waving her arms, and pointing in the direction of Ocean View, down the coast.

"Who in the world will understand that?" demanded Mollie.

"Allen will," answered Betty.

"Oh!" exclaimed Mollie with a laugh. "Then this isn't the first time you have talked with him in sign language."

"Silly!" protested Betty. "Come on, girls," and she strode off down the wet sands. The rain had almost stopped.

"This is better than waiting back in that hut," observed Mollie, walking beside the Little Captain.

"I should say so!" exclaimed Betty. "Oh, those horrid faces."

"Just like smugglers!" declared Mollie.

"What's that about smugglers?" demanded Grace, quickly, turning around. She was in advance with Amy.

"Oh—nothing," spoke Betty, and Grace resumed her talk with her other chum.

The girls walked along the beach. Now a turn of the coast hid the boys from sight, and their work of towing back the drifting motor boat.

"Oh, it's farther than I thought!" sighed Grace, as the atmosphere became clearer, and, some distance down the coast they could see the little village of Ocean View.

"Oh, it isn't far at all!" declared Betty. "We haven't done enough walking lately, that's the reason. We'll soon be there."

As the girls made a turn around some high sand dunes they heard the staccato puffing of a motor boat.

"Can that be the boys?" asked Mollie, quickly.

"Of course not! They are away behind us," declared Betty, "and that sound came from in front. See, there it is—a motor boat," and she pointed to one just leaving the shore of a little cove.

Several men had evidently just leaped into the craft which, because of the shallow water, had to be shoved some distance out.

Then a strange thing happened. The men appeared to be surprised at the sight of the girls—an unexpected sight, it would appear—for some of them seemed anxious to put back, while others were urgent for keeping on out into the bay.

"That's queer!" commented Betty.

"What?" asked Amy.

"Those men seem anxious to come back; at least, some of them do, and others don't," went on Betty. "Look, they seem to be quarreling among themselves!"

CHAPTER IX

THE BOX IN THE SAND

"Goodness!" cried Grace, shrinking back against Betty. "They are fighting!"

"It does look so," responded the Little Captain. "One man seems to be trying to jump overboard!"

It did so appear to the outdoor girls. The motor boat containing the half-dozen rough-looking men was rapidly leaving the shore of the cove, but one man in it seemed anxious to return to the beach. His companions had forcibly to restrain him, as he seemed willing to leap into the water, and swim back.

Confused shouts and cries came from the men in the boat, as though they were of several opinions. Finally, however, the majority seemed to gain their point, and the man who had appeared so excited quieted down.

But, as the boat gathered headway, this man, sitting in the stern, never took his eyes from four girls. He watched them until the craft was so far out that his features could not be distinguished.

"Wasn't that odd?" demanded Amy, being the first to speak after the little episode.

"It certainly was," agreed Betty.

"They seemed afraid—yes, actually afraid of us," put in Grace.

"And there wasn't the least need of it," laughed Mollie. "I wouldn't have harmed one of those men—oh, for anything!"

"I guess not!" Amy declared. "I was all ready to run if they headed their boat back this way."

"What in the world do you suppose was the matter?" asked Grace, as they stood looking after the vanishing boat. The boys were no longer in sight, being hidden from view behind a projecting point of land.

"Perhaps this is private grounds we are on," suggested Mollie, "and they didn't like to see us trespassing."

"It couldn't have been that," Grace remarked. "Everyone walks along the beach, and I believe no one is allowed to claim any land below high water mark, so it couldn't have been that."

"Maybe there are quicksands here!" exclaimed Amy, looking nervously about. "There are such things, you know. The Goodwin Sands, in England, are awful. If you once are caught in a quicksand you never get out."

"Nothing like that around here," asserted Betty. "If there was, you can depend on it, Daddy never would have hired a cottage."

"Besides," added Grace, "if there had been danger the men would not have been in two minds about coming back to warn us. They would surely not have let us run into danger."

"No, it couldn't have been that," decided Betty. "But the men were certainly divided in opinion about coming back here, and they must have left just before we came in sight. Well, it will never be solved, I suppose, but I don't know that it need worry us. Though if the boys were here I think they would make quite a mystery of it."

"Will would make quite a fuss about it, if he were here, I guess," laughed Grace. "He'd be sure the men were pirates, or something like that, show his new badge and want to question them."

"Then I'm glad he isn't here!" exclaimed Amy, with such warmth that Grace exclaimed:

"Oh, Amy! I never knew you cared—so much."

"I don't! That is—yes, of course I care! That is—oh, I wish you'd let me alone!" burst out the blushing Amy, whereas Grace teased her all the more, until Betty put an end to it saying:

"Well, let's get along. The men don't seem to be coming back, and mamma may be worried, knowing that we went out when a storm was brewing. Old Tin-Back is sure to tell her that we went off defying the elements."

"Isn't he a queer old character?" remarked Mollie.

"Yes, but I like him," Betty answered. "He says he has never yet given up hope of finding some treasure washed ashore from a wreck. He's always looking as he walks along the beach."

"And that in spite of the fact that, with all his years of looking, he has found only a pipe," laughed Mollie. "He is very persevering, is Old Tin-Back."

"Most fishermen are," spoke Betty.

"I suppose things *are* occasionally washed up by the sea," Amy observed. "Let's look as we walk along the beach."

Hardly knowing why they did so, the eyes of the outdoor girls roamed the beach, which, as the tide had just gone out, was strewn with odds and ends. Nothing of moment, though, it seemed—bits of broken boxes and barrels, bottles and tin cans, probably the refuse from coasting vessels.

"Oh, I'm tired!" suddenly exclaimed Grace. "Let's see if we can't find a place to sit down."

"Tired! No wonder, wearing such high-heeled shoes!" objected Betty. "You are violating one of the ethics of the outdoor girls' organization!" she went on. "You can't expect to walk in those."

"I'm not going to try again," confessed Grace. "Oh, I simply must sit down."

"The sand is so wet," objected Mollie.

They managed to find a broken spar, cast up by the waves, and by putting on it some boards, which they turned over to find the dry side, they evolved a comfortable seat.

"Oh, isn't this just lovely!" exclaimed Betty, as she gazed out over the bay, now glistening beneath the sun, which had come out from behind the storm clouds.

"It is perfect," agreed Amy.

Mollie was idly digging in the sand behind the spar. She used a shell, and had scooped out quite a hole. Suddenly the shell scraped on something with a shrill sound.

"Oh, don't!" begged Grace. "You set my teeth on edge! What is it, Mollie?"

Mollie did not answer at once. She was digging in the sand more quickly now. Again the shell scraped on some metal.

"Oh, Mollie!" objected Grace again, putting her hands over her ears. "What is it?"

"I—I think I've found something," replied Mollie in a low voice. "Look, girls, it's some sort of box."

They leaned over her. Her shell had scraped away the wet sand from the top of a square piece of metal. Mollie tapped it.

"It—it sounds hollow!" she whispered.

"Probably a tin can," said Betty.

"No," spoke Mollie, resolutely.

"Here, let me help you!" exclaimed Amy.

She looked about for something with which to dig. Near where Mollie had uncovered the piece of metal a queerly shaped stick stuck upright in the sand. Amy pulled it out, with no small effort, and at once began digging.

"Oh, it's some sort of a box—an iron box!" cried Mollie, with eager, shining eyes. "We have really found something."

Mollie and Amy dug until they had wholly uncovered the object. Then, with a quick motion, Mollie put her hands under the lower edges, and with a sudden effort brought up out of the hole in the sand a curious iron box.

"It—it really is—something!" she said.

Instinctively Betty looked out over the bay in the direction taken by the strange, quarreling men in the motor boat.

CHAPTER X

CONJECTURES

Mollie Billette set the black iron box down on the log that had formed the seat for the outdoor girls. A little wind was rapidly drying the dampness. The wind even dried some of the sand on the box, and scattered it in a little rattling shower on a bit of paper on the beach.

The girls did not seem to know what to say. Betty looked back from her glance across the bay, in the direction of the now unseen boat, in time to notice Mollie, ever neat, wiping her damp hands on her pocket handkerchief. Amy was looking at the queerly-carved stick which had served her as a shovel to dig in the sand.

"Oh! Oh!" exclaimed Grace. "Isn't it wonderful! It really is a box!"

"Yes, it's certainly *that*, all right!" added the more practical Mollie.

"And if it should contain treasure!" went on Grace, rather at a loss because her chocolates were all gone.

"Old Tin-Back should have found this," commented Mollie.

"Or the boys," spoke Betty. "I wish they were here."

"The idea!" exploded Mollie. "As if we didn't know what to do as well as though the boys were here to tell us. That isn't our Little Captain; is it, girls?" she asked the others.

"Oh, I only meant about the legal end of it," said Betty, quickly.

"Oh, I see! She just wants—Allen!" remarked Grace.

"No, it isn't that at all!" Betty cried, quickly. "But you know there are certain rules about things found at sea, or near the sea. For instance, if this is above the high-water mark it might be, the property of whoever owns the land back there."

"Well, it's above high-water mark all right," declared Amy. "Though I think in a heavy blow or at a high tide the water might come up here. But we can't go by rules now; can we, Betty?"

"Oh, I suppose not."

"I'm going to take the box home with us," Mollie declared. "It may have been washed ashore from some ship, and there may be nothing in it but——"

"Tobacco!" exclaimed Grace with a laugh.

"Tobacco?" questioned the others in a chorus.

"It looks just like a tobacco box," the chocolate-loving girl went on. "But perhaps it isn't."

"Of course it isn't!" declared Mollie.

"I'm sure it contains treasure," said Amy. "Oh, if it should! Wouldn't the old lobsterman be surprised?"

"Well, he wouldn't be the only one to be surprised," spoke Mollie.

"I think we would ourselves," added Betty, with a laugh. "Now, girls, let's see what we really have found."

With a bunch of seaweed Mollie brushed from the box the sand that clung to it. Then the outdoor girls gathered around the case as it rested on the log.

"Look!" exclaimed Grace as the covering of sand was disposed of. "There are some letters on the box."

"So there are!" agreed Betty. They leaned forward to look.

Staring at them from the black top of the box were three white letters. They were rather scratched and faded, but the girls soon made them out as follows:

B. B. B.

"B-B-B," repeated Mollie, as she read them. "I wonder what they stand for?"

"Base-ball-band," said Grace, quickly. "At least that's what Will would say if he were here."

"I wish some of the boys *were* here," remarked Betty, and again she gave a quick glance out across the bay.

"Why?" Amy wanted to know.

"Because those men might come back, and——"

"Do you think those men hid the box here?" asked Grace.

"That's exactly what I think," replied Betty, quickly. "Wouldn't that be an explanation of their strange conduct when they saw us?"

"How do you mean?" asked Amy.

"I mean I think those men had just hidden this box here in the sand. As they went away they saw us coming along. They were afraid we would find the box, or at least some of them were, and wanted to come back to dig it up again."

"And do you think that was why they quarreled among themselves?" demanded Mollie.

"I think so—yes. Doesn't it seem natural?" Betty asked.

"Well, of course you can make almost any theory fit when you don't know the facts," Mollie went on. "But how about the box having been washed up from the ocean, and buried in thesand naturally? That could have happened; couldn't it?"

"Oh, yes," assented Betty. "The box wasn't buried so deep but what it could have come about in a perfectly natural way. But when you stop to think how the men acted, and the fact that it was just about here their boat was, I think my idea is the best."

"Well, it certainly was from here they pushed off their boat," declared Grace, walking down toward the edge of the water. "See, there are the marks of the keel in the sand."

That was true enough, as all the girls could see. The black box had been buried in the sand directly back from the point where the men had made their departure.

"There's another thing, too," added Betty. "That stick Amy has."

The other girls looked at it, Amy herself regarding it with rather curious eyes.

"It was stuck in the sand near the box," Amy said. "I worked it loose, pulled it up, and used it as a shovel."

"Exactly what it might have been intended for," spoke Betty, who let a little note of exultation creep into her voice. "At least, that was one of the purposes for which it was intended."

"And what was the other?" Mollie asked, as she put back a stray lock of her dark hair, for the wind had blown it about.

"As a mark," said Betty.

"A mark!" exclaimed Amy.

"Yes," went on Betty. "The men who hid the box put the stake in the sand so they could find their treasure again."

"Oh, then you are sure it *is* treasure," Mollie returned.

"Well, we might as well think that as anything else—until we get the box open and find it full of—sand!" declared Betty, laughing.

"Oh, let's open it now!" cried Grace, impulsively. "I'm just dying to see what's in it. Please let's open it now."

"Perhaps we have no right," objected Amy.

"Why, of course we have," insisted Grace, making "big eyes" at Amy. "We found it. Can't we open it, Betty?"

But there was a very good reason why the girls could not open the box—at least then and there.

CHAPTER XI

THE CIPHER

"Locked!" exclaimed Betty, laconically, when she had tried the cover of the box.

"Oh, dear!" came petulantly from Grace. "Isn't that horrid!"

"Well, I suppose the men have a right to lock up their treasure," coolly remarked Betty, again vainly trying to raise the cover.

"You will have it that those men hid the box," said Amy, with a smile. "Also that it is treasure."

"I'm getting romantic—like Grace," commented the Little Captain.

Then, as they found that their efforts to open the box were vain, the girls looked at it more closely.

It was a black japanned box of tin, or, rather, light sheet iron, rather heavier than the usual box made for holding legal papers. It was such a receptacle as would be described, in England, as a "dispatch box." And in fact, the box didseem to be of some foreign make. It was not like the light tin affairs used locally to hold deeds, insurance policies and the like.

The cover fitted on tightly. This much was seen at a glance, and so well did it fit that it needed a second look to make sure which was the bottom and which the top, for there was no bulge or "shoulder" of the metal to indicate where the lid rested.

"It's water-tight, I'm sure," Mollie said, when the box had again been set upright. They decided that the top was that place where the initials "B. B. B." showed, half-obliterated, in white paint.

"Then it might have been washed ashore from some wreck," Amy said.

"Too heavy to float," was the answer of Mollie, as she again lifted it.

"But it could work up in a heavy wind or sea; that is, if it didn't go down too far from shore," Grace remarked. "But can't we get it open some way?"

"We might break it," Mollie observed. "Otherwise, I don't see how we can. It is a complicated lock, if I am any judge," and she looked at the front of the box. "Let me take that stake, Amy."

"Oh, no! Don't break it open!" expostulated Betty. "We must try and see if we can't slip the lock, after we get it home. Papa has a lot of odd keys."

"But I don't see any lock!" exclaimed Grace.

"There it is," and Betty pushed to one side a round disk of metal that fitted over the keyhole.

Whether this was to keep out sand or water, the girls could not determine. It might even have been designed to hide the keyhole, but former use, or the battering which the box had received, had loosened and disclosed the metal slide, and Betty's quick eyes had discerned the object of it.

"It would take a peculiar key to open that," decided Mollie. "Mamma has a historic French jewel case home, and it has a lock something like that."

"Oh, suppose this contains—jewels!" cried Grace. "Wouldn't it be just—"

"Nonsense!" broke in Betty. "If the box contains anything at all it is probably papers of no value. My own opinion is that there's nothing in it, for it's too light. However, we'll take it home, and see what the boys say."

"You seem to have a great deal of faith in their opinion," laughed Mollie. "Ah, my dear!" and she put a finger on Betty's blushing cheek. "Methinks it is the opinion of one certain boy you want."

"Silly!" murmured Betty.

"Oh, don't mind us. A legal opinion would be most excellent to have," mocked Grace. "Now who is eating the chocolates?" she wanted to know.

Betty did not answer. She bent over the black box, with its indefinable air of mystery, and the three queer letters on the top. She was, seemingly, trying to find a way to open it.

Finally she straightened up, looked once more across the bay and said:

"Well, let's take it to Edgemere."

"And let's hurry, too!" urged Amy.

"Hurry? Why?" asked Grace. "There's no more danger from the storm."

"No, but those men might come back, and, finding their treasure gone—oh, well, let's hurry," she finished.

"Don't make me nervous," begged Grace, with a glance over her shoulder. "Come along, Betty. I'm just dying to see what is in it. But I'm not so sure those men in the boat left it, and if they demand it don't you give it up to them."

"Oh, I should say not!" cried Mollie, bristling a bit. "We found the box. They'll have to prove ownership."

Betty tucked the box under her arm. No one disputed her right to carry it, for the other girls deferred to the Little Captain in matters of this sort.

"Won't the boys be surprised when they see it!" commented Amy.

"But listen!" cautioned Betty. "We mustn't pretend that we think there is anything in it. If we do, and there isn't, they'd have the laugh on us."

"Oh, of course," assented Grace. "We'll just say we found the box on the beach, and couldn't open it. The boys will be anxious enough to do that."

And, sure enough, when the girls reached the cottage, the boys being not far behind them, the latter were even more eager than Betty and her chums to have a look inside the mysterious iron case.

"Pry the cover off!" cried Will, when he and the others had briefly related their experience in saving their motor boat and sailing back in the other craft, while the girls gave their story bit by bit, from the sighting of the men in the boat, to the finding of the box. Only Betty said nothing about the faces at the window of the fisherman's hut.

"Pry the cover off!" cried Will. "An axe is the best thing to use!"

"Indeed not!" exclaimed Betty. "Let's see if we can't open it with a key. You have some odd ones; haven't you, Daddy?"

"Yes," assented Mr. Nelson, who was down at the shore for the week-end. "Betty, get them. You'll find them in that desk in the living room."

Betty's father had looked at the box on all sides, had shaken it, and had examined the lock through a reading glass.

"It sure is a find, all right!" declared Roy Anderson. "I wish I had been with you."

"Oh, if it's a treasure-trove, we'll all share, as they did in Treasure Island," declared Betty, who was almost a boy in her liking for adventure stories.

"Ahem!" exclaimed Allen Washburn, with an elaborate assumption of dignity. "Treasure, you know, is subject to the claim of the commonwealth, if the lawful heirs cannot be located. I must look up the law on that subject."

"More likely it's the spoil of pirates, and fair booty for whoever finds it!" declared Will. "I think I'm the proper one to take charge of this, representing as I do the United States Government, which takes precedence over any State commonwealth."

"Go on!" laughed Henry Blackford. "You'll be saying next that it's smugglers' booty, and you'll be asking us to pay a duty on it. Let's open the box and see what it is—maybe nothing but seaweed. I've heard of jokes being played before," and he looked at the girls meaningly.

"Oh, we didn't hide it and then find it again," Amy assured him, so earnestly that the others laughed.

"Well, here goes for a try, anyhow," said Mr. Nelson.

With a bunch of assorted keys he tried one after another in the strange lock. Some keys would not even enter the aperture, while others turned uselessly around in it.

Betty's father used all he had without success, and then the boys were called on. They were not able to produce the Sesame to the japanned box, and Will's plan of using an axe was finding more favor when Allen produced a small key of peculiar make.

"Try this," he said. "It locks the switch on the motor boat, but it may fit. It looks as though it would."

And, to the surprise of them all, it did. As though it had been made for that lock, the little switch key slipped in. There was a click, a grinding sound, as the cover slipped on the sand-encrusted hinges, and the lid went back.

"Stung!" cried Roy, as nothing was seen but a slip of paper within the black interior.

Mr. Nelson lifted it out.

"I can't make anything of this," he said. "It's some sort of a note, written in cipher, I should judge. It is signed 'B. B. B.'"

"The same letters that are on top of the box," said Allen.

"Was there ever a pirate who had those initials?" asked Mollie, and the others laughed. "Well, there might have been," she went on. "I don't think it's so funny."

"Of course it isn't, dear," declared Betty. "I guess we're all a bit nervous. Is that all there is, Daddy?"

"Everything, my dear. The box is empty save for this bit of paper that doesn't make any sense."

"We must translate that at once, sir," said Allen. "If it is in cipher that's all the more evidence that it means something. I might have a try at that secret message, or whatever it is."

"Well, you're welcome to have a go at it," assented Mr. Nelson. "It may all be a joke, so don't take it too seriously."

"I'll not," agreed Allen.

He took the paper from Mr. Nelson's hand. The others looked over his shoulder at it.

"Oh, what do you suppose it means?" marveled Grace. "Do hurry and translate it, Allen."

CHAPTER XII

THE FALSE BOTTOM

For a moment the queer box itself was forgotten in the wonderment over the cipher. That it would prove a solution to the mystery, if such there was, and that it was not a joke, was believed by all. Even Allen, calm as he usually was, displayed some excitement. The girls themselves could not conceal their eagerness.

"How are you going to make sense out of that?" asked Roy, who did not like to spend much time over anything. "It's worse than Greek."

"Most ciphers are," agreed Allen. "The only way to translate it is to go at it with some sort of system. I'll need plenty of paper, and some pencils."

"I'll tell you what to do," said Mr. Nelson. "Make several copies of the cipher, and we can all work on it at once. It will be a sort of game."

And a fascinating game it proved. The possibility that the queer paper in the iron box might contain directions for finding some hidden treasure made it all the more alluring.

"There are any number of ciphers," Allen explained, when several copies had been made of the original. "The simplest is to change the letters of the alphabet about, using Z for A, and so on. Another simple one is to make figures stand for letters, as No. 1 is A, and so on. But those are so simple that only a schoolboy would use them."

"What are same of the more difficult ciphers?" asked Betty.

"Well, there are so many I don't know that I could explain them all. But the most simple of the difficult ones is the taking of a number of arbitrary signs or symbols to represent the letters of the alphabet. That is what was done in Poe's 'Gold Bug,' you remember. Unless the person has a copy of the list of signs and symbols it is very difficult to decipher that cipher, or decode it, as they say in government circles."

"Ahem!" exclaimed Will, with an important air, as all eyes were turned on him. "I ought to know something about that, but you see they haven't trusted me with the code book yet. Now then, Allen, how are we to go about this Chinese puzzle?"

"If I had that story of Poe's here, it would be rather easier," Allen said. "As it is, we shall have to do a little preliminary work. To start off with we will take the letter E."

"Why E?" asked Roy.

"Because of all the letters in the ordinary use of English, that letter most frequently occurs," Allen answered. "In other words, if you take a written, or printed, page, and count up the letters, you will find that E is used most frequently."

"What is the next one?" asked Mollie. "Oh, isn't this fascinating, girls!"

"It will be more fascinating to discover the secret," Betty said.

"I don't know what letter is next in importance, or, rather frequency," Allen answered. "But we will each take a book and by counting the letters on a page we can find out."

"Some work!" groaned Roy. But they began it. Even Mr. and Mrs. Nelson were interested enough in the novel game to attempt it.

It took some little time, but at last Betty and Allen, who were working together, announced that they found A to be the next most predominating letter after E. And the others' search agreed with this. Then in order came o, i, d, h, n, and so on.

But they did not do that in one day, or even two, for they found it rather tiring to the eyes. So that it was not until three days after the finding of the box that Allen was ready with the ground-work of his cipher translation.

In the meanwhile the motor boat had been repaired and was ready for service. The weather had cleared, and in the intervals of working over the mysterious paper in the box the boys, escorted by the girls, went to the place where it had been found. The hole in the sand was just as they had left it.

"The men haven't come back to discover their loss," said Betty.

"Or, if they have, they are leaving the ground undisturbed with a view to getting a clue to the one who took the box," Allen said, with a look at Betty.

The next day a real attempt was made to decipher the code. As Allen had said, it was made up of several letters, numbers and arbitrary signs, some of them resembling Chinese characters in form.

"The thing to do," said Allen, "is to pick out the letter, number or sign that occurs most frequently. In other words, the predominating one. And that will be E, for E is the predominating letter in any communication. Now we'll begin."

They all had great hopes, but, alas! they were doomed to disappointment. For either Allen's system was wrong, or else the cipher did not follow the plan of any of the well known ones. They succeeded in deciphering it, after a fashion, but the result was a meaningless jumble of words that told them nothing. The word "treasure" did not even occur; that is, according to the translation made by Allen.

"Well, I give up," he said, with a sigh of disappointment. "I sure thought I could make something of it, but I can't."

"Maybe Will could send it to some of his Secret Service friends," suggested Grace.

"Yes, I could do that," her brother assented. "Let's let the government experts take a crack at it, Allen."

"I'm willing," assented the young lawyer.

Betty was in a corner of the big sitting room, the bay window of which gave a beautiful view of the ocean. She had the queer box in her lap, and was turning it from side to side, now and then holding it to her ear and shaking it.

"What are you doing, Betty Nelson?" asked Grace, coming in from a walk to town.

"I was just listening to see if there was any hidden mechanism in this box," answered the Little Captain. "I wonder if there's a ruler anywhere about?" she went on.

She found a foot ruler, and with that began measuring inside and outside the box, jotting down some figures on a piece of paper.

"What's this—a new way to work out the cipher I couldn't solve?" asked Allen, coming in.

"Don't talk to me for a minute, please," said Betty, puckering up her forehead.

She seemed to be adding and subtracting, and then she suddenly cried:

"I thought so! I thought so! It is the only way to account for the thickness of it."

"The thickness of what?" asked Allen.

"The bottom of that box!" went on Betty. "It has a false bottom. I'm sure of it. Look here! It is seven inches deep on the outside, and only five inches deep inside. Where are those two missing inches except in a false bottom?"

In her excitement Betty tapped on the inside of the bottom of the box with the ruler, and then a strange thing happened.

There was a clicking, springing sound, and the bottom of the iron box seemed to rise up in two parts, like the twin doors of a sidewalk elevator hatchway. The false bottom had been found, and as it swung up out of the way there was disclosed an opening in which lay a package wrapped in white tissue paper.

"Oh! Oh!" cried Betty, staring at the box "I—I've found it—the treasure!"

CHAPTER XIII

THE DIAMOND TREASURE

For a moment the others clustered around Betty like bees in a swarm, saying not a word. The girls could only gasp their astonishment as they looked over the Little Captain's shoulder, as she sat there, holding the black box, the false bottom of which had so unexpectedly opened before their eyes.

The boys were a little more demonstrative.

"How in the world did you do it, Bet?" asked Will.

"Did you know there was some trick about the box?" demanded Roy.

"She's been holding this back," declared Henry, nudging his sister Amy.

"And to think of all the time we wasted on that cipher!" observed Allen, reproachfully.

This seemed to galvanize Betty into speech.

"I didn't know a thing about it!" she declared, earnestly. "I just discovered it by accident. Of course when I found there was a difference in depth between the inside and the outside of the box I began to suspect something. But I didn't dream of—this!"

She motioned to the white package in the secret compartment—a package she had not, as yet, touched.

"But how in the world did you come to discover it, Betty dear?" asked Mollie, with wonder-distended eyes.

"It seemed to open itself," the Little Captain replied. "I just dropped the end of the ruler in the box, and it sprang open."

"You must have touched the secret catch, or spring," was Allen's opinion.

"Let's have a look!" proposed Will. "I always did want to see how one of those hidden mysteries worked. Pass it over, Betty!"

"Indeed, don't you do it!" cried Mollie. "Let's see, first, what is in that package, Betty. You said it was a treasure; didn't you?"

"Well, that's what I said," admitted Betty. "But it will probably be some more meaningless cipher."

"Oh, do open it!" begged Grace. "I'm all on pins and needles——"

"Thinking it may be—chocolates!" teased her brother.

She aimed a futile blow at him, which he did not even dodge.

Betty reached in and lifted the white tissue-paper package from its hiding place. It almost completely filled the space. There was a rustling sound, showing that the paper had acquired no dampness by being buried under the sand in the box.

"Put it on the table," suggested Allen, removing the box from Betty's lap. She turned to the table, near which she had been sitting, when her experiment resulted so unexpectedly. On the soft cloth she laid the paper packet.

"Now don't breathe!" cautioned Mollie, "or the spell will be broken."

No one answered her. They were all too intent on what would be disclosed when those paper folds should be turned back.

"It looks just like—just like—pshaw! I know I've seen packages just like that before, somewhere," said Will. "But I can't, for the life of me, think where it was."

"Was it in a jeweler's window?" asked Amy, in a low voice, from where she stood beside him.

"That's it, little girl! You've struck it!" Will cried, and impulsively he held out his hand, which Amy clasped, blushing the while.

"What's that talk about a jeweler's?" asked Allen.

But no one answered him.

For, at that moment Betty had folded back the white paper, and there to the gaze of all, flashing in the sun which glinted in through an open window, lay a mass of sparkling stones. Thousands of points of light seemed to reflect from them. They seemed to be a multitude of dewdrops shaken from the depths of some big rose, and dropped into the midst of a rainbow.

"Oh!" cried Betty, shrinking back. "Oh!" She could say no more.

"Look!" whispered Grace, and her voice was hoarse.

"Well, I'll be jiggered!" gasped Will.

"Diamonds!" cried Allen. "Betty, you've discovered a fortune in diamonds!"

"Diamonds?" ejaculated Amy, and her voice was a questioning one.

Then there came a silence while they all looked at the flashing heap of stones—there really was a little heap of them.

"Can they really be diamonds?" asked Betty, finding her voice at last.

Allen reached over her shoulder and picked up one of the larger stones. He held it to the light, touched it to the tip of his tongue, rubbed it with his fingers and laid it back. He did the same thing with two others.

"Well?" asked Will, at length. "What's the verdict?"

"I'm no expert, of course," Allen said, slowly, and he seemed to have difficulty in breathing, "but I really think they are diamonds."

"Diamonds? All those?" cried Mollie. "Why, they must be worth—millions!"

They all laughed at that. It seemed a relief from the strain, and to break the spell that hung over them all.

"Hardly millions," spoke Allen, "but if they are really diamonds they will run well up into the thousands."

"But are they really diamonds?" asked Betty.

"As I said, I'm no expert," Allen repeated, "but a jeweler once told me several ways of testing diamonds, and these answer to all those tests. Of course it wouldn't be safe to take my word. We should have a jeweler look at these right away."

"I knew I had seen paper like that before," Will said. "It's just the kind you see loose diamonds displayed in around holiday times in jewelers' windows."

"That doesn't make these diamonds, just because they are in the proper kind of paper," scoffed Roy. "I think they're only moonstones."

"Moonstones aren't that color at all," declared Henry. "They are sort of a smoky shade."

"I guess Roy means rhinestones," said Amy, with a smile.

"That's it," he agreed. "They're only fakes. Who would leave a lot of diamonds like that in a box in the sand?"

"No one would leave them there purposely, to lose them," said Allen. "But I think we've stumbled on a bigger mystery here than we dreamed of. I am sure these are diamonds!"

"I—I'm afraid to hope so," said Betty, with a little laugh.

"Well, it's easy to tell," Allen said. "There's a jeweler in town. He probably doesn't handle many diamonds, but he ought to be able to tell a real one from a false. Let's take one of the smaller stones and ask him what he thinks."

"Oh, yes, let's find out—and as soon as we can!" cried Grace. "Isn't it just—delicious!"

"Delicious!" scoffed Will. "You'd think she was speaking of—chocolates!"

CHAPTER XIV

SEEKING CLUES

The first shock of the discovery over (and it was a shock to them all, boys included), the young folks began to examine the stones more calmly. They spoke of them as diamonds, and hoped they would prove to be stones of value, and not mere imitations.

There were several of fairly large size, and others much smaller; some, according to Allen, of only a sixteenth-karat in weight.

"But stones of even that small size may be very valuable if they are pure and well cut," he said.

"And what would be the value of the largest ones?" asked Betty, for there were one or two stones that Will was sure were three or four karats in size.

"I'd be afraid to guess," Allen said. "We'd better have them valued."

The girls handled the stones, holding them on their fingers and trying to imagine how they would look set in rings.

"Engagement rings?" asked Grace of Betty, who had suggested that.

"Silly! I didn't say anything of the kind!"

"Well, it isn't what you say, it's what you mean."

It did not seem they could look at the stones enough. Every specimen was examined again and again, held up to the light, and turned this way and that in the sun so that the sparkle might be increased.

"Well, I suppose we might as well put them away," said Betty, with a sigh, after a while. "It's no use wishing——"

"Wishing what?" demanded Mollie, quickly.

"That they were ours."

"Ours! I don't see why they aren't!" exclaimed Grace, quickly. "Of course Mollie and Amy dug them up, but——"

"Oh, don't hesitate on my account!" Mollie said, quickly. "If we share at all we share alike, of course."

"That's sweet of you, Billy," returned Betty. "But I don't see how we can keep them. The diamonds, if such they are, must belong——"

"Yes, whom do they belong to?" demanded Mollie. "If you mean the men we saw in the boat, I should say they didn't have any more right to them than we have. They were pirates if ever I saw any."

"Well, you never saw any pirates," remarked Betty, calmly. "But of course the men in the boat may have hidden the diamonds there."

"Do you think they knew they were in the box?" asked Amy.

"Well, whoever hid the box must have known it contained something of value," Betty declared. "They would hardly hide an empty box, and if they had found it locked they would have opened it to make sure there was nothing of value in it. Of course those men may only have been acting for others."

"But what are we to do?" asked Amy.

"We must try to find out to whom these diamonds belong," Betty said. "We'll have to watch the advertisements in the paper, and if we see none we'll advertise for ourselves. That's the law, I believe," and she looked at Allen.

"Yes, the finder of property must make all reasonable efforts to locate the owner," he said, "though of course he could claim compensation for such effort. I think the papers are our best chance for finding clues.

"Has there been a big diamond robbery lately?" asked Mollie.

"What has that to do with it?" Will wanted to know.

"Because I think these diamonds are the proceeds of some robbery," went on the girl. "As you say, the stones are wrapped in a paper just as though they had come from a jewelry store. It might be that those men broke into a store, took the diamonds and hid them in this secret part of the box, which one of them owned. They are probably from some big robbery in New York, or Boston, seeing we're nearer Boston than we are New York, up here."

"I don't remember any such robbery lately," Roy said, and he was a faithful reader of the newspapers. "But of course we've been pretty busy lately. I'll get some back numbers of the papers."

"Ha! What's going on now?" asked the voice of Mr. Nelson. He had come in from the station, having run up to Boston on business.

"Oh, Daddy!" cried Betty. "Such news! You'll never guess!"

"You've solved the cipher!" he hazarded.

"No. We didn't need to. We solved the mystery of the box, and look——"

She spread the sparkling stones out before him.

"Whew!" he whistled. "I should say that was news. Where did you get those?"

"In a hidden compartment of the black box. I stumbled on the secret spring by accident when I was measuring it. Are they diamonds, Father?"

Anxiously the young people hung on Mr. Nelson's answer.

He laid aside the packages he had brought from Boston, and turned for a moment to greet his wife, who had come into the room. She had been told of the find as soon as it was discovered, and had been properly astonished.

"It takes the young folks to do things nowadays," he said, with a smile.

"Doesn't it?" she responded.

"But are they diamonds? That's what we want to know!" chanted Betty, her arms around her father's shoulders.

Mr. Nelson tested the stones much as Allen had done, but he went farther. From his pocket he produced a small but powerful magnifying glass. It was one he used, sometimes, in looking at samples of carpet at his office. He put one of the larger stones under the glass.

The young people hardly breathed while the test was going on. But the result was not announced at once, for Mr. Nelson took several of the sparkling stones, and subjected them to the scrutiny under the microscope.

"Well," he announced finally, "I should say they are diamonds, and pretty fine diamonds, too!"

The girls gave little squeals of delight.

"You were right, old man," spoke Henry to Allen, with a nod.

"Well, I wasn't sure, of course" began the young law student "but——"

"Of course I didn't look at all the stones," broke in Mr. Nelson, and the talk was instantly hushed to listen to him, "but I picked several out at random, and made sure of them. And it is fair to assume in a packet of stones like this that, if one is a diamond, the others are also."

"And how much are they worth?" asked Betty. She was not mercenary, but it did seem the most natural thing to ask.

"Well, it's hard to tell," her father replied. "At a rough guess I should say—oh, put it at fifty thousand dollars."

"Oh!" cried Mollie. "To think of it!"

"Catch me! I'm going to faint!" mocked Roy, leaning up against Will.

"Do you really think they are as valuable as that?" asked Amy, in a gentle voice.

"She helped find them, and she wants to reckon her share," said Mollie, who did not always make the most appropriate remarks.

"Nothing of the sort!" exclaimed Betty. "It's just the wonder of it all."

"I think fifty thousand dollars would be pretty close to the mark," said Mr. Nelson. "I once had to serve on a committee to value the contents of a jewelry store for an estate. I didn't know much about precious stones, but the others gave me some points, and I remember them. Of course I may be several thousands out of the way, but——"

"Oh, fifty thousand dollars is a nice enough sum—to dream about," Betty said, with a gurgling laugh. "It will do very well, Daddy dear."

"But isn't it the most wonderful thing, that we should find all those diamonds!" gasped Mollie.

"Who could have hidden them?" wondered Amy.

"That's what we've got to find out," put in Allen. "I suggested the newspapers," he went on to Mr. Nelson.

"And a good idea," that gentleman said.

"Oh, Betty. Let's look at the box, and see how the wonderful false bottom fitted in," proposed Mollie. "I think it was the most perfectly gorgeous thing how you happened to discover it."

"And that's just how it was—a happening," the Little Captain remarked. "Oh, but if those men in the boat should discover that we have those diamonds, and come for them," and Betty glanced nervously over her shoulder.

"Ha! Let them deal with *me!*" exclaimed Will, as he displayed his Secret Service badge. "I'll attend to the—pirates!"

"I thought your specialty was—smugglers," voiced Allen, with a chuckle.

"Smugglers or pirates, it is all one to me!" Will declaimed, strutting about.

"Oh, but——" began Betty.

"Well, what?" Will asked. "Think I'm afraid?"

"No—oh, no. I was thinking of something else."

And to Betty came a vision of those glowering faces in the window of the fisherman's hut on the beach.

CHAPTER XV

A NIGHT ALARM

The diamonds were wrapped again in their protective covering of tissue paper. The girls could hardly take their eyes off them as Mr. Nelson put them in his pocketbook.

"Oh, it doesn't seem—real," sighed Betty, with a long breath.

"No, it is like some fairy story," agreed Mollie. "And to think the box has been in the house two or three days, and we never knew what a treasure it contained."

"Because of that secret compartment," suggested Amy. "Wasn't it just wonderful?"

That same false bottom of the tin box was interesting the boys more, just then, than were the diamonds themselves. Will, Allen, Roy and Henry gathered around the queer jewel casket.

"There, it's shut!" exclaimed Will, as a click proclaimed that he had pushed the two folding leaves of sheet iron back into place. "You'd never know but that that was the real bottom," said Roy.

"Let's see if we can open it again," proposed Allen.

The boys tried, pushing here and there. But the bottom did not fly up as it had done for Betty.

"Say, what magical charm, or 'Open Sesame,' did you use on this?" asked Allen, after vainly trying. "We can't make it work, Bet."

"I don't know," she answered. "I just simply jabbed it with the ruler, that's all."

"Well, then, please 'jab' again," pleaded Will.

Obligingly Betty took the piece of wood, and began poking about in the bottom of the tin box. For some time she was as unsuccessful as the boys had been.

"I don't believe I can do it again," she said, puckering her forehead in an attempt to remember. "Let's see, I sat *this* way, and I held it *that* way."

"Did you have your fingers crossed?" asked Roy, laughing.

"What had that to do with it?" demanded Betty. But before Roy could answer she uttered a cry, for, as she was moving the ruler about on the bottom of the box, there was that sudden click and spring again, and the false bottom sprang out of the way, disclosing the place where the diamonds had been.

"How did you do it Betty?" asked Allen, and then it was seen that the ruler had pressed on a tiny plate in the corner of the box, a plate so well hidden that only the most careful scrutiny revealed it.

Once it was seen, however, the trick was easy to work. The cover was snapped into place again, and as soon as the ruler, or for that matter, the tip of one's finger, pressed on the little plate, the hiding place was disclosed.

The boys and girls "played" the trick over and over again, until it was an easy matter to do it.

"This is more fun than the cipher," said Allen, taking a copy of it from his pocket.

"Going to have another go at it?" asked Will.

"Yes. It might be a clue to the owner of the diamonds."

"That's so," agreed the other. "I would like to know to whom they belong."

"I suppose diamonds are smuggled once in a while; aren't they?" asked Allen.

"Indeed they are," Will answered. "That's what Uncle Sam has to guard against more than anything else. They are so easy to hide, and it doesn't take many of them to represent a whole lot of money. But then the government has the system down pretty fine, and it isn't often that anything gets away. You see as soon as any purchase of stones on the other side is made, word is sent to the officials here—that is, any purchase of any large amount, such as this."

"Then you don't think those diamonds were smuggled?" asked Allen.

"Not for a minute!" declared Will. "They're the proceeds of some robbery, all right. I'm sure of that. Smugglers don't work the game that way—bury the stuff in the sand. It's a robbery!"

"Well, perhaps you're right," assented Allen, as he bent over the cipher.

"I'll have another go at that with you," said Will, as he looked over his copy.

But the further efforts of the boys, and the girls, too, to decipher the code, were unavailing. The queer paper held fast to its mystery, if indeed mystery it concealed. It did not give it up as had the box with the secret bottom.

The day when the diamonds were discovered was an exciting one, and the excitement had not calmed down when evening came. Mr. Nelson had taken charge of the precious stones, and it had been decided not to say anything about them, even to the servants in the house.

"And I don't believe I'd take one to the village jeweler," was the opinion of Betty's father. "As a matter of fact, I don't believe he would be any better judge of the stones than I am, and he certainly would talk about them."

"That's right," Mollie agreed. "The folks here want to know what you had for breakfast and what you're going to eat for luncheon and dinner. I suppose they can't help it."

"No, the natives haven't much to do," affirmed Betty, "except to talk about the summer cottagers. But we'll keep quiet about the diamonds, at least down here."

"If the natives only knew what we know!" exclaimed Grace. "Think of having dug up buried treasure from the sand!"

"Poor Old Tin-Back would be heartbroken if he ever heard of it," said Amy, gently. "All his life he has dreamed of finding treasure, or ambergris or something, and here we come along and take it right from under his eyes."

"Poor old man," sighed Betty. "He is a dear, and so honest. He brought some crabs to-day, hard ones, for the shedders aren't around yet. And he was so careful to have every one alive. He held them up for me to see them wiggle."

"I can't bear them!" exclaimed Grace, making a wry face.

"You mean uncooked," observed Mollie. "I notice you take your share when the salad is passed."

"Oh, well, that's different," Grace returned.

"What are you going to do with the diamonds?" asked Betty of her father, when they were gathered around the sitting room table, after supper.

"I haven't fully decided," he said. "I want to make some inquiries in Boston, first, as to whether or not there has been a robbery."

"That's what I'll do, too," said Will.

"When are you going to Boston?" asked his sister. "First I heard about that."

"I'm going up in the morning," her brother answered. "I received word to report at the office. There's something that needs my attention. Ahem! Uncle Sam can't get along without me, it seems."

"Nothing like patting yourself on the back," Grace said.

"Just for that you sha'n't have any of—these!" and Will drew from his pocket a box that unmistakably held candy.

"Oh, Will. I didn't mean it!" Grace cried. "Of course you're of value to the government. What are they—those new bitter-sweets?"

"That's for you to ask, and Amy to know," said Will, as he passed Amy the confections.

"Oh, thank you!" she said, blushing furiously.

"Amy Blackford. What I know about you!" mocked Mollie.

"Oh, I'm going to share them, of course."

"Oh, of course!" chanted Grace. "How nice."

"Well, it will keep her still for a while, at least," sighed Will.

"Whom do you mean?" demanded Mollie, catching him by the ear.

"Ouch! Let go! I meant my sister—of course. A fellow wouldn't dare talk that way about anyone but his sister," confessed Will.

Merrily they discussed the finding of the diamonds, and what disposition might be made of them. The strange actions of the men in the boat, too, came in for a share of attention. The girls were quite sure the men had hidden the box in the sand, though whether or not they knew of the valuable contents was a question.

"Well, they'll look in vain for it now," declared Betty. "We have it," and she glanced at the now empty receptacle.

"Better put it away," suggested her father. "If the servants see it they may ask awkward questions."

"I'll keep it in my room," said Betty.

"And I'll have another go at this cipher to-morrow," Allen said. "I have a new idea for solving it."

"I thought you were going to take us girls out in the boat to-morrow," objected Mollie.

"So I am. But I can be working on this between times."

"Sorry I can't be with you," Will said.

"Then you are really going to run up to Boston?" asked Mr. Nelson.

"Yes, sir, I have to go, if I want to keep this new position."

"Well, I'd advise you to do so, then. Go up with me on the express in the morning."

"Thank you, I will."

"And if you hear anything about the diamonds, don't wait to come back and tell us, write—no, telegraph!" urged Betty.

"It wouldn't be wise to wire," her father objected. "There is no great rush. I will make some inquiries myself."

"And where will you leave the diamonds, meanwhile?"

"Down here, of course. I'm not going to carry them around with me—too valuable," and Mr. Nelson patted his pocket.

"I'll take the box to my room, and lock it in my trunk," Betty said.

The evening wore on. It was one of beautiful moonlight, and the party of young people went out on the beach to have a marshmallow roast over a drift-wood fire.

"The sea sparkles—just like diamonds," said Mollie, as they turned to go back to the cottage, when the little frolic had ended.

"Hush!" cautioned Betty. "Some one might hear you," and she looked out over the bay as though she might catch a glimpse of the rough men in the boat.

"You have diamonds on the brain," chided Grace.

The cottage became quiet. Only dim night lights burned. Betty had taken to her room the queer box, which had given up part of its secret. Her father had the diamonds with him.

It was Grace who gave the alarm. Awakening at she knew not what hour, and feeling the need of a drink of water, she donned a dressing gown and found her slippers. As she went through the hall to the bathroom, she saw a dark figure, unmistakably that of a man, gliding down the corridor. Under his arm was the black box, and in one hand was held a tissue paper packet.

"The diamonds!" screamed Grace, her voice shrilling out in the night. "Burglars are after the diamonds!"

CHAPTER XVI

ON THE BEACH

The whole house was roused in an instant. Lights gleamed in various rooms, and from the quarter where the maids slept came shrill screams that matched those of Grace herself. Hoarse shouts came from the rooms of the boys.

But the affair had a most unexpected ending. For the man at whose back Grace was gazing horror-stricken, turned at her sudden shout, and his face betrayed almost as much astonishment, not to say fear, as the countenance of the girl showed.

And then Grace noticed that the man was attired in a bath robe, the pattern of which was strangely familiar to her. She noticed this even before she looked at his face recognizingly, and beheld her host, Mr. Nelson.

"Oh! Oh!" gasped Grace, weakly, and she had to lean against the wall for support, for she was trembling.

"What—what's the matter?" asked Betty's father. "Are you ill, Grace?"

"No, but I—I thought you—oh, I thought——"

Out into the hall poured the others of Edgemere Cottage, attired in a nondescript collection of garments hastily donned. Will, in his bath robe, had his collar and tie in his hand, though it is doubtful if he wore an article of dress to which it could be attached. From the servants' rooms came frantic demands to know if the house were on fire.

"No, it's all right!" called Mr. Nelson. "Go back to bed, all of you!"

"But what's it all about?" asked Betty. "What is the matter?"

"Oh, I guess it's my fault," Grace said. "I got up to get a drink, and I saw your father going down the hall, with the box and the package of diamonds, and I thought—I thought he was a——"

"Burglar! Is that what you thought me?" demanded Mr. Nelson, as a smile crept over his face.

"Ye—yes," faltered Grace. "I know it was silly of me—dreadfully silly, but I—I——"

"It's all right, my dear. I don't blame you a bit!" comforted Betty, her arms around the shrinking figure of Grace. "Go on back, you boys!" she commanded the others. "Our—our hair isn't fit to be seen!" and the boys retired, snickering. No girl likes to be looked at in a dressing gown, when suddenly aroused from sleep. And one's hair doesn't appear half so becoming in that state as it does even under a bathing cap.

"But what does it all mean?" asked Mrs. Nelson, who had waited to put on something smarter than a dressing sack before venturing out into the hall.

"Grace thought papa was a burglar," explained Betty.

"Well—that is, I didn't exactly——" protestingly began Grace.

"Did you have a nightmare?" asked Mrs. Nelson. "I'm afraid the diamond excitement was too much for you. A little bromide, perhaps, or some——"

"Oh, she doesn't need that," Betty said as the boys "made themselves small" around a corner, that they might hear the explanation, if unseen. "She really did think papa was taking the diamonds."

"Why, he is!" cried Mrs. Nelson, as she caught sight of the objects her husband carried—the mysterious box and the packet of precious stones. "What are you doing with them?" she asked.

"I was putting them in a safer place," he explained. "Perhaps it was foolish of me, but, after I had brought them to my room, I got to thinking it was rather careless to leave them about so. It wasn't so much the fear of thieves as it was of fire. You know diamonds can't stand much fire."

"Oh, if they should be melted before we know who owns them!" gasped Mrs. Nelson.

"So when I found I couldn't sleep, for thinking of them," went on Betty's father, "I made up my mind to hide them in a different place. Perhaps it was foolish of me, but I couldn't help it. I'm as bad as some of the girls, I guess," and he glanced at Betty and her chums, who now, with flushed cheeks and looking pretty enough for any number of boys to gaze upon, even if their hair was a bit awry, stood grouped in the hall.

"So I got up," resumed Mr. Nelson, "took the diamonds from the bureau drawer where I had placed them, and started to take them down cellar. I——"

"Down cellar!" cried Betty. "What a place to hide diamonds—in the cellar!"

"It's the safest all-around place," her father said. "I don't believe any burglars would be able to find them where I was going to put them, and in case of fire the diamonds would be in little danger. Of course they might be buried under a lot of rubbish, but they wouldn't go up in puffs of smoke.

"So I got up as quietly as I could, and took the diamonds, intending to go down cellar with them, hoping I would disturb no one."

"But where did you get the box?" asked Betty. "That was in my room, Daddy."

"I know. I went in and took it out."

"And I never awakened?"

"No."

"A fine guard for the diamonds," mocked Will from around the corner of the hall.

"Go to bed—you boys!" commanded Betty.

"I thought I would take the box, too," Mr. Nelson resumed. "It forms one of the clues, and I didn't want anything to happen to that. So

I decided to take that, put the diamonds in the secret bottom, and hide all down cellar. Only Grace rather upset my plans."

"I—I'm so sorry," said the thirsty one, contritely.

"Don't you be!" returned Betty. "You're as good as a watch dog. To think of me never waking when papa came in my room."

"I was glad you didn't," he said. "I hoped to have it all go off quietly, and tell you in the morning. But as long as you know it now I might as well proceed. I'll go on down cellar and hide them."

"And don't forget to tell us where you put them," Betty urged. "If you go away in the morning, we'll want to know where to run to get them in case the house does catch fire."

"Oh, don't suggest such a thing!" begged her mother.

Mr. Nelson laughed and went on down cellar, coming back soon to tell the waiting ones that he had found a little niche in the wall, near the chimney, and had put the diamonds in the box there. Then the house quieted down again.

Will and Mr. Nelson left on an early train for Boston, both promising to do all they could to learn the secret of the mysterious package of diamonds.

"And now what shall we girls do?" asked Betty, after breakfast.

"What do the boys want to do?" queried Mollie. "Perhaps you may have some plans for us."

"Sorry, ladies," Allen said, "but our boat is on a strike again, and we'll have to have it fixed. It isn't much, though, and we can go out this afternoon."

"Then we'll go down on the beach for a while," proposed Betty. "It's lovely this morning. We'll go in bathing just before luncheon, and then, after a little sleep, we'll be ready to have the boys amuse us."

"Sounds nice, to hear them tell us," commented Roy with a laugh.

And this plan was followed. When the boys went off in the motor boat, the ignition system of which was not working to their satisfaction, the girls strolled down to the shore, walking along it.

"Let's go as far as the place we found the diamonds," proposed Amy.

"Think you might find some more?" asked Betty, with a smile.

"No such luck. But I thought perhaps we might see——"

"Those men again? No, thank you!" cried Grace.

"Nonsense!" exclaimed Mollie. "The beach is free, and it is broad daylight. Come along."

So they strolled along the sand, stopping now and then to pick up a pretty shell or pebble. Out in the bay was the fleet of clamming boats, little schooners from which the grappling rakes were thrown overboard, and allowed to drag along the bottom with the motion of the craft, to be hauled up now and then, and emptied of their shelly catch.

On the other side of the point of land the ocean beat restlessly on the beach.

"Here's the place," exclaimed Betty, at length, as they came to the log where they had sat when Mollie and Amy dug up the box of diamonds.

"It doesn't look as though they had come back and searched in vain for the treasure," said Betty.

There was no evidence in the sand, that was certain. The girls looked about a bit, and then strolled on. Before they knew it they found themselves in front of the lone hut where, from the odor that hung in the air, and the evidence of nets and boats about, it was evident a fisherman dwelt.

As the girls came opposite this, the door opened and a woman, with a hard, cruel face, peered out.

"Ah, little missies!" she croaked, "it's a fine morning for a walk, but you must be tired. Won't you come in and rest?" And she leered up into their faces.

CHAPTER XVII

ANOTHER ALARM

At the first sight of the old crone Betty had drawn back, and now, as the fishwife spoke, in a voice which she tried to render melodious, though it ended only in a croak, the Little Captain seemed to urge her chums away.

"What does she mean?" whispered Grace.

"Come in and rest—it is wearyin' work, walkin' in the sand," the woman persisted. "I know, for many a day I have walked it lookin' for my man to come back from the fishin' channel. But he's away now, and it's lonesome for an old woman. Do come ye in!"

"No, thank you, we like to be out of doors," answered Betty, forestalling something Amy was going to say.

"I could give you a drink of milk," the old fishwife went on. "Nice cold milk. And cookies I baked myself—molasses cookies."

"No, thank you just the same," spoke Betty, in a voice she tried to render appreciative, though she showed a distinct distaste for the nearness of the old woman. "We have just had breakfast," she added.

"But won't you come in and rest?" the crone persisted. "The walk in the sand——"

"No, we aren't tired," said Mollie, seconding Betty's efforts. "And we must be going back. Come on, girls. I'll race you to the old boat!" she cried, with a sudden air of gaiety, and she set off at a rapid pace.

For a moment the others hung back, and then Betty cried:

"Come on, girls! It sha'n't be said that Billy beat me!"

The old woman stared after the girls, uncomprehendingly for a moment, and then, with a scowl on her face, turned back to the hut again.

"Run on! Run on!" she muttered. "But I'll get ye yet! I'll get ye!"

She turned, and seeing the backs of the girls toward her, shook a gnarled and wrinkled fist at them.

"I'll get ye yet!" she repeated.

As she entered the hut a man's face was thrust down through an opening in the ceiling—a hole that had been covered by a hatch-board.

"Wouldn't they come?" he asked.

"Naw! They turned from me as if I was dirt."

"The snips! Well, maybe we'll get another chance."

"Another chance?" repeated the crone.

"Yes! We've got to, I tell you. If not, Jake will——"

"Hush! No names!" cautioned the woman.

Meanwhile the outdoor girls, having raced to the goal, an old boat half-buried in the sand, came to a panting halt. Mollie had won, chiefly because she had started off before the others, for Betty was accounted the best runner of her chums.

"Well, what does it all mean?" asked Grace, who came limping in last, for, in spite of her expressed promise to the contrary, she still wore those high-heeled shoes. "You act as though you had run away from the plague, Betty!"

"And so we did, my dear. The plague of fish! Ugh! I can almost taste them—fishy, oily fish!"

"And she offered us—milk!" added Mollie.

"It would probably have been—cod-liver oil," spoke Betty, with a shudder of repugnance. "Oh, let me get a breath of real air!" and she turned her face to the misty wind of the sea.

"But what does it all mean?" asked Amy, in rather bewildered tones. "Why did we run away?"

"That's what I want to know," put in Grace. "And I believe—yes, I have dropped my chocolates. Oh, how provoking! I'm going back after them."

"You're going to do nothing of the sort!" declared Betty, with a firmness she seldom manifested.

"But—why?" questioned Grace. "Why can't I go back after my candy?"

"Baby!" mocked Mollie.

"Because it's probably near that abominable hut!" said Betty. "And that old crone might capture you. Did you see how eager she was to get us in there?"

"She did seem rather insistent," agreed Amy. "But was it any more than mere kindness?"

"If you ask me—it was," said Betty, firmly.

"But why?" persisted Grace.

"Eternal question mark!" Betty commented. "Now, girls," she went on, "I don't know all the whys and wherefores, but I'm sure of one thing, and that is nice people don't live in that hut. I don't mean just poor, or unfortunate, or ignorant people, either," she went on. "I mean they aren't nice—or—or safe! There, perhaps you'll like that better."

"Not safe?" repeated Grace. "What do you mean?"

"I mean I saw faces looking from the window of that hut, the day we found the diamonds, that I wouldn't want to meet in the dark, or alone—those who go with the faces, perhaps, I should say."

"Oh!" exclaimed Grace, glancing involuntarily over her shoulder.

"Oh, no one is following us," Betty said; "but I wanted to get well away."

"Why do you think she wanted us to go in?" inquired Mollie.

"Do you think it had anything to do with the diamonds?" was Amy's question.

"I don't know what to think," confessed Betty. "But I wouldn't have gone into that hut for a good bit. Though perhaps the worst we would have been asked would have been to purchase some worthless trifles."

"Or perhaps buy smuggled lace," suggested Mollie.

"I never thought of that!" exclaimed Betty. "Of course it might be that."

"If Will were only here!" said Amy.

"We'll tell him when he comes back," Betty said. "Perhaps it may not amount to anything, but if he can give the government some information it may serve him a good turn, since he is just beginning work in the Secret Service."

"But do you really think that old woman, and those you may have seen through the window of the hut the day we made our find, have anything to do with the diamonds?" asked Mollie.

"Frankly, I haven't the least idea," admitted Betty. "And what is the use of guessing and wondering? Only I am sure of one thing. I'll never go into that hut!"

Betty little realized how her boast was to be recalled to her under strange circumstances.

The outdoor girls sat down to rest on the old boat, and talked of many things. The impression caused by the old woman's invitation soon wore off. Then they started back, for they wanted to get their morning bath before luncheon.

"Oh, some one is here!" exclaimed Betty, as they saw an auto standing on the graveled drive of the cottage. "I wonder who it can be?"

"You father or Will wouldn't be back so soon; would they?" asked Amy.

"No, it must be——"

A voice interrupted Betty.

"Ah, I dare say I shall find them! I will keep along the beach. Charming weather, isn't it? Ah, yes, really!"

"Percy Falconer!" said Grace. "Catch me, somebody!"

"Hush! He'll hear you!" cautioned Betty, and a moment later the "johnny" of Deepdale, attired in the latest fashion in motoring togs, came out on the porch, followed quickly by Mrs. Nelson.

"Oh, here are the girls now!" said Betty's mother.

"Yes," assented Betty. "We are back," but there was no enthusiasm in her voice.

"Oh, but I say, I am charmed to see you—all," added Percy, after a glance at the Little Captain. "I motored down, don't you know. Father let me, after some arguing. I should have liked to come in the boat, with the rest of the fellows, but I can't stand the sea, really I can't. But I'm glad I'm here."

"Yes, we—we are glad to see you," Betty said. "We are going in bathing; won't you come along?"

"Ah, thank you, now. I'm afraid it's a little too cool for going into the water to-day; don't you?"

"No, we like it!" said Mollie. "How did you leave Deepdale?"

"Oh, everything is the same, though it's very lonesome, with you girls away."

"Oh, who let him in?" murmured Grace, with a despairing glance at Betty.

"Hush!" the latter cautioned her. "At least he has his car, and we can have a ride now and then," for Mollie's machine was in use by her mother that summer, and the girls had no chance at its pleasures.

"Mercenary!" whispered Mollie to the Little Captain.

Percy was made as welcome as the circumstances permitted, and he sat on the sand under a huge umbrella while the girls frolicked in the water. The boys came back for luncheon, and helped to divide the boredom of the newest arrival, though they made uncomplimentary remarks behind his back, and Betty was in constant fear lest some unpleasant incident should occur. She had to remember that she was the hostess.

Nothing was said of the incident at the fisherman's hut, and that afternoon the young people went for a motor boat trip. That is, all but Percy Falconer. He could not be induced to embark, even on the calm waters of the bay, and so he spent a lonesome afternoon at the cottage, talking to Mrs. Nelson.

Toward evening Betty found a chance to speak to Old Tin-Back, who came with a mess of crabs.

She asked him who lived in the little, lone hut.

"Well, no one as you would care to know, Miss Betty. He's a man that hasn't a good name."

"A man? But I thought a woman——"

"Oh, yes, Mag, his wife, is there, too. She's worse than Pete in some respects."

"Are they smugglers?" Betty wanted to know.

"Well, they might be, if there was anythin' to smuggle. But I call 'em just plain—thieves. Pete could tell lots about other folks' lobster and crab cars being opened if he wanted to, I guess."

A telegram came from Mr. Nelson that evening, saying he would remain in Boston two or three days. He added that there was "no news," which the girls took to mean he had heard nothing about the diamonds. Will sent no word.

It was about nine o'clock, when, after a stroll down the moonlit beach, the boys and girls were returning to the cottage. As they came up the walk a scream rang out.

"What's that?" cried Allen, who was beside Betty.

"It sounded like Jane, the cook," was the answer. "But——"

More screams interrupted Betty, and then the voice of a woman was heard calling:

"Come quick! There's men in the cellar!"

CHAPTER XVIII

ANXIOUS DAYS

"Come on, boys!" cried Allen, evidently the first to sense the meaning of the alarm.

"Oh, but shouldn't we have some sort of weapons, you know?" spoke Percy.

"Get out of my way!" cried Roy Anderson, brushing past the dude. "My fists are the only weapons I want."

Betty and the other girls hung back in a frightened group. The maid's voice continued to ring out, and now Mrs. Nelson could be heard demanding to know what was the matter.

"Around to the side, fellows!" commanded Allen. "There's an outer door they'll probably try for."

"But who'll guard the front here?" asked Amy's brother.

"Let Percy do that!" Allen flung back over his shoulder. "He probably won't come with us, anyhow," he added.

The three young men hastened around to the side of the cottage, while Percy, hardly knowing what to do, remained with the girls in front. At the side was an old-fashioned, slanting cellar door, the kind celebrated in song as the one down which children slide, to the no small damage of their clothes.

As Allen and his chums reached a point where they could view this door, they saw it suddenly flung up with a bang, and three men spring up the stone steps.

"There they are!" yelled Roy.

"After 'em!" shouted Henry Blackford.

"It wasn't a false alarm, anyhow," added Allen. "Hold on there!" he cried. "Stop! Who are you? What do you want? Stop!"

But neither the commands nor the questions halted the men. They ran on, with never a word of answer or defiance flung back— dogged shadows fleeing through the moonlight to the shrubbery-encompassed grounds of Edgemere.

"Stop, or I'll shoot!" cried Roy.

"Oh!" screamed Grace, covering her ears.

"Good bluff, all right," complimented Allen. "But it won't work."

Nor did it. Roy's bright idea went for naught, for the men still crashed on. They were lost sight of now behind a screen of bushes, but the boys were not going to give up the pursuit so easily.

"Come on!" called Allen. "We'll have them in another minute! They can't get over the stone wall."

"Stone wall?" echoed Henry.

"Sush! It was another bluff, just as my threat was to shoot," cautioned Roy. "It may turn them back."

But it did not. Evidently the men knew the grounds about Edgemere as well as did the boys, for there was no sign of a halt in their headlong pace. On they crashed through bushes and underbrush, dodging among the trees of the garden, and minding not the flower beds they trampled under foot.

"They're getting away from us," remarked Henry, who was panting along beside Allen.

"Yes, they evidently had a line of retreat all marked out."

"Who are they?"

"Haven't the least idea. Tramps, maybe—maybe something worse."

"You mean——"

"I don't know just what I do mean," replied Allen. "Come on, let's do a little sprint, and we may get them. If we don't they'll soon be down on the beach, and it will be all up with[the chase if they have a boat, as they probably have."

"If it was on the ocean side we'd have some chance; the surf is heavy to-night."

"Yes, but they're running toward the bay."

As I have explained, Edgemere was built on a point of land. One side of the house fronted the ocean, and the other the bay. At this point the land was not above a thousand feet wide, and the cottage property extended from shore line to shore line.

As Allen had said, the intruders, coming from the cellar, had turned toward the bay side, and if they had a boat waiting for them in those quiet waters they would have no difficulty in pushing off. But if they had gone the other way the unusually heavy surf would have held them back, at least for a time.

"There they go!" cried Roy, breaking out through the last fringe of bushes.

"And in a motor boat, too!" added Roy.

"If we only had ours," Henry mourned.

But it was vain wishing. The *Pocohontas* was docked some distance away, and by the time the boys could reach her, and start an engine that was never noted for going without considerable "tinkering," it would be too late.

For the men had luck on their side. They fairly tumbled into a swift looking craft that was near shore, in charge of some one evidently waiting for them. In another instant the chug of the motor told that it had started. Then the boys had the dissatisfaction of standing on the sand, panting after their run, and seeing the men gradually draw out into the bay.

The sky had clouded over and the moon, that might have been a help, was not now of any service.

"Well, there they go," said Allen, in exasperated tones. "I'd give a good deal to know who they were, and what they were after."

"Let's go back to the house and see if we can find out," suggested Roy. "The fuss started there, you know."

"In the cellar—where the diamonds are," added Henry.

"That's so!" cried Allen. "For the moment I had forgotten them! Come on back. Maybe the rascals got the stones!"

The boys went back the same route they had so recently and so uselessly traveled. As they neared the cottage a voice hailed them.

"I say. Hold on! Who are you? What do you want? Remember there are ladies here!"

"It's Percy!" gasped Allen, trying not to laugh. "He's acting as home guard!"

"I wonder if he has his wrist watch on," laughed Roy.

"It's all right," called Henry, not wishing his sister and the other girls to be needlessly frightened. "We're coming back."

"Did you get them?" asked Betty, from the darkness.

"No, they got away in a boat," answered Allen. "Is anyone hurt?"

"No, but the servants and mother are quite frightened. Could you see who they were?"

"No. Evidently tramps, or fishermen. We'll have to have a look at those——"

Allen did not complete the sentence, but they all knew to what he referred.

"So you—er—missed them?" questioned Percy, when the two groups were together again. "Too bad! I was just coming to join you. I had to have a weapon, you know, and I found—this."

He showed a little stick which he had picked up.

"I should have hit them with it had I gotten near enough," he went on, seriously—for him.

"It's a good thing you didn't," spoke Roy. "You might have killed one of them with that, Percy."

"Oh, so I should! I—I can strike very hard when I am angry. I am just as well pleased that there was no need for desperate measures. I really am!"

But no one paid any attention to him now, though he tried to walk beside Betty. Allen and Roy had taken this vantage place, one on either side of the Little Captain.

"Betty, where are you?" called Mrs. Nelson, from the darkness.

"Here, Mother. Don't worry. It's all right. The men got away in a boat. We are coming in to hear all about it."

The story was soon told.

One of the maids, going down cellar to get something from the food store-room, had surprised a man prowling about with an electric flashlight.

The girl screamed, and her cries were augmented by the yells of another domestic in the kitchen.

Then the first girl saw two other men come from some part of the cellar and join the first one. They ran out just as the boys came up, and the fruitless chase resulted.

"What sort of men were they?" asked Betty of the girl who had given the alarm.

"Oh, I don't know, Miss Betty," was the half-sobbed reply.

"But you must know! Did he wear a tall hat or——"

"A tall hat? Of course not, miss. He was like a tramp, or a fisherman—maybe a clammer."

"That's how I sized them up," Allen said. "Fishermen. Did they say anything to you?" he asked the maid.

"Not a thing—no, sir. He just caught his breath, sort of frightened like, and ran out."

"Did the one you saw call to the others?"

"Oh, no, sir, they all ran out at once, as soon as I went down. I had a light myself."

"What part of the cellar were they in?"

"I couldn't exactly say. They seemed to be all over."

"Well, we'll have a look for—to see if anything is missing," Allen hastily changed his remarks, for the servants knew nothing about the diamonds; or, at least, they were not supposed to know about them.

"Come on, boys," the young law student went on.

"Oh, but hadn't we better send for the authorities?" asked Percy. "Or at least take a weapon," for Allen and the others had nothing in their hands.

"He's loony on the subject of weapons," grunted Roy.

Allen led the way down cellar, the girls and the servants not venturing, though Betty did want to go. But her mother kept her back.

A glance served to show that the diamonds were in the box, safe. As far as could be learned the intruders had not been near them.

"We'll bring them up, after the servants have gone to bed," Allen confided to his chums.

And when the maids had retired there was a sort of "council of war" among the others.

Opinion was divided as to whether the men were ordinary tramps, or perhaps sneak thieves, or whether they were after the diamonds.

"But how would they know they were down cellar?" asked Betty. "We are the only ones who know of the hiding place, and we haven't told anyone, except Percy."

"Oh, I never said a word!" Percy cried. Indeed he only heard the story of the find, after the scare.

"Of course if some men from this neighborhood hid the diamonds in the sand, and knew we girls took them out, and if they were around the house and heard something of the excitement the night papa took them down cellar, it would explain how they knew where to look for them," Betty said.

"Too many ifs," commented Allen. "Have there been any strangers around lately—tramps or anyone like that?"

At first Betty said there had been none, but later she recalled that a maid had reported to her that an undesirable specimen of a man had begged something to eat at the kitchen door the morning after Mr. Nelson had hid the diamonds down cellar.

"And," Betty said, "he may have been hanging around when father and Will left for Boston that day."

"But how could he know the stones were hidden down cellar?" asked Mollie.

"I don't know that he could tell that, exactly," Betty admitted, "but if you remember, as papa was going away he called back: 'Be sure to keep the cellar locked!' Don't you remember?"

"Yes, I heard that," Amy contributed.

"Well, if a tramp, who was not really a tramp, but some one in disguise, heard that he might jump to some conclusion," Betty went on.

"Too much jumping," Allen said. "As a matter of fact we're all in the dark about this."

"And it isn't a very pleasant suspense, either," declared Betty, as she looked at the black box with the diamonds safe in the secret compartment. "What are we going to do with that?"

"Hide it in a new place," suggested Henry.

That much was decided on, and the treasure was taken up to the attic, though there the danger of fire was ever present.

"Oh, I wish father were home," said Betty, a worried look on her face.

But it would be several days before Mr. Nelson could return, and those days were anxious ones indeed for the outdoor girls. The morning after the scare in the cellar inquiries were made, but no trace of the mysterious men was found.

"I can't stand this much longer!" declared Betty, one night. "I almost wish we'd never found the diamonds."

"You're nervous," said Mollie. "We've been too much in the house. To-morrow we shall try one of our old stunts—a picnic!"

"Good!" cried Grace. "That will be fun!"

CHAPTER XIX

THE PICNIC

"Did you bring plenty of olives?"

"And I do hope we didn't forget the cheese crackers!"

"Oh, everything is here—more than we'll eat, I think, by the weight of the baskets."

"Where did I put—oh, here they are!"

This last, with a sigh of relief, as she found her package of candy, came from Grace. Mollie, Amy and Betty had, in turn, been heard from in the aforequoted remarks.

"It's a glorious day; isn't it?" questioned Grace as she walked on beside Amy.

"Yes, but not so nice that you need forget you're carrying only a box of chocolates," remarked Betty, pointedly. "Take one of these baskets."

"Oh, excuse me," apologized Grace, and she turned quickly, wincing a bit as she did so.

"Those same ridiculous shoes!" cried Mollie.

"You ought to be ashamed of yourself, Grace Ford."

"Why? They're the most comfortable ones I have, to go tramping about in, and they're so stained from the salt water that they can't be damaged any more. Just right for the picnic, I think."

"Yes, but you walk worse than a Chinese woman before the binding of feet was forbidden. Don't let her carry anything spillable, Betty, or we won't have all the lunch we count on," Mollie urged.

"Oh, is that so!" exclaimed Grace, with as near an approach to "snippiness" as she ever permitted herself.

"Oh, I'll carry the basket," said gentle Amy, always anxious to avoid a quarrel.

"You'll do nothing of the sort!" insisted Betty, who had, like the Little Captain she was, arranged the commissary department on lines she intended to see carried out.

"Oh, well, if we're going, let's go!" exclaimed Mollie. "We're wasting the best part of the day getting ready."

It was the day after Mollie had proposed that the outdoor girls go on a little picnic, and her plan had been enthusiastically adopted. As she had said, the affair of the diamonds was getting on the nerves of them all. They had stuck too close to the house, and there was a "jumpiness" and fault-finding spirit seldom manifested by the four chums.

They were to take their lunch, and spend the day on the beach, or in the scrubby woods, not far away, taking to a boat if they felt so inclined.

The boys had offered to take them out for a cruise in the *Pocohontas*, but the girls felt that they would rather be by themselves on this occasion.

Accordingly lunch baskets had been packed and now this glorious summer morning they were about to start. The boys, their kind offer refused, had gone off on a fishing jaunt—that is, all but Will, and he had not returned from Boston. Grace had a hasty note from him in which he stated that work connected with his new duties would keep him busy for a week or so, after which he hoped to join his friends at Edgemere.

"No news of a diamond robbery around Boston," he wrote, in a letter. "I've written to a fellow in New York about it, though. Sometimes the police keep those things out of the papers for reasons of their own. Maybe they think the robbers won't know the diamonds have been taken, if nothing is printed about it, at least that's the way it looks."

At any rate Will reported no news, and Mr. Nelson had pretty much the same story to tell. His wife had written to him about the men in the cellar, and he had advised getting some fisherman of the neighborhood to stay on guard every night, until he could come down to Ocean View again.

"We might get Old Tin-Back," suggested Betty.

"It would only make me nervous," her mother said. "I don't believe the men will bother us again."

"Well, they won't find the diamonds down cellar if they do pay us another visit," Betty had said. She had, after some thought, hidden the precious stones in her own room, wrapping the box in some sheets of asbestos, which Allen had left over after putting some on the muffler of the motor boat.

"The asbestos will protect the diamonds in case of fire," Betty said, "and I'll protect them in case of thieves. Anyhow, no one, not even the servants, know where they are, and it would take a good while to find them in my room."

For she had discovered an ingenious little hiding place for the mysterious black box.

The boys, after the scare of the men in the cellar, had offered to take the diamonds up to Boston, or some other city near Ocean View, and put them in the vault of some bank.

"But you might be robbed on the train, going up," objected Betty. "We'll keep them here until the secret is discovered. That will be the best thing to do."

"And that may never be," Allen had said, for he had long since given up the cipher. Nor had experts, to whom he had submitted it, been able to furnish a clue to its solution.

So, while the boys had gone out fishing in the motor boat, the girls prepared for their picnic, leaving the diamonds at home.

Percy Falconer had declined the boys' invitation to go fishing, and when Betty heard him say that he feared to go out on the water she had looked at her chums with hopeless despair on her face.

"What if he wants to come on the picnic with us?" she whispered to Grace.

"We—we'll run away from him!" had been the ultimatum. But Percy did not pluck up enough courage to trust himself, the only youth, with four girls.

"I'll go for a run in my car, and may pick you up and bring you back later," he said, with a glance at his wrist watch. He was still a guest at Edgemere.

"Well, let's start!" called Betty, and the four girls set off down the beach.

"Why are you going that way?" asked Grace, as Mollie and Betty, who had taken the lead, started along a certain path amid the sand dunes.

"Just for fun," answered Betty. "I have a fancy for looking again at the place where we found the diamonds."

"We can't seem to get rid of them, day or night—sleeping or waking," spoke Amy. "Isn't it dreadful how they follow one?"

"Well, I, for one, don't want to get rid of them," Mollie said, with a laugh. "They are far too pretty and valuable to lose sight of. Though of course I want whoever owns them to get his property back."

"Even those horrid men?" asked Grace.

"Well, if they have a right to the diamonds, the fact of their being horrid, as you call it, should not deprive them of the stones," Betty said.

"We ought to get a reward, anyhow," spoke Amy.

"That's right, little girl!" exclaimed Betty. "Well, I do wish it was settled, one way or the other. Having fifty thousand dollars' worth of diamonds, more or less, in one's possession isn't calculated to make one sleep nights. And I justwould love one of those big sparklers in a ring. I think——"

But Betty did not complete her sentence. There was a rattling sound on the farther side of a sand dune around which the girls were just then making their way. Some gravel and shells seemed to be sliding down the declivity.

"What's that?" asked Grace, shrinking back against Betty.

"I don't know," answered the Little Captain. "Maybe the wind."

But it was not the wind, for, a moment later, the wrinkled face of the aged crone of the fisherman's cabin peered at the girls from over the rushes that grew in the sand hill.

"Oh, excuse me, my dears," she said in her cracked voice. "I didn't see you. Out for a walk again; aren't you, my dears? Won't you come up to my cottage, and have a glass of milk?"

"No, thank you," Betty answered, and she could not help being "short," as she said afterward. "We are going on a little picnic."

She swung around into another path between the dunes, and changed her mind about going to look at the hole near the broken spar, where the diamonds had been found.

"Oh, I wonder if she heard us?" whispered Mollie, as they lost sight of the old crone around the rushes and dunes.

"I hope not," said Betty, and her usually smiling face wore a worried look.

CHAPTER XX

CAUGHT

"That woman seems to—persecute us!" burst out Mollie, when the girls were well on their way again, out of range of the sand dunes, going down the beach where the salty air of the ocean and bay blew in their faces.

"Oh, hardly as bad as *that*," remarked Amy.

"Well, she always seems to be following us," insisted Mollie, "and I am positively tired of being asked to her cottage to drink milk."

"I'd never touch a thing she offered," said Betty. "I would be afraid it wouldn't be—clean."

"She always seems to leer at one so," went on Mollie.

"Oh, you're making out a terrible case against the old woman," Grace put in, carefully selecting a chocolate from her supply.

"Well, she is very persistent," observed Betty. "And now let's forget all about her, and the—well, I won't mention them, but you know what I mean," and she smiled at her chums. Indeed Betty was beginning to think she had been just a little indiscreet in speaking aloud of the precious stones.

"We'll just have a good outing, as we used to," she went on.

"Like the time when we found the five-hundred-dollar bill," suggested Amy.

"Or when the girl fell out of the tree," added Mollie.

"Gracious! Those were tragic times enough!" broke in Grace.

"But we enjoyed them—after they were over," added Betty. "And I think we shall enjoy finding—well, finding what we did find, after Allen straightens it out for us."

"Oh, is he going to straighten it out for us?" asked Mollie.

"Well, isn't he working hard on it?" Betty wanted to know.

"I thought Will was going to get us clues," Mollie went on. "Or your father?"

"Oh, of course they may find the owners, but they are waiting for something to be published in the papers."

"Well, is Allen doing any more?" Amy asked. "If he is he hasn't said anything to us about it, though of course you'd be the first one to hear of it, Betty," she said, innocently enough.

"I?" cried the Little Captain, with upraised eyebrows. "Why I, pray?"

"Oh, because you and Allen are——"

"That's enough!" laughed Mollie. "Spare her blushes, child!"

"Oh!" exclaimed Amy, in confusion.

"You needn't worry about me," said Betty, quickly. "What I meant was that Allen is working on a plan to solve the mystery."

"Has he told you all about it?" Grace wanted to know.

"Not all. We agreed that it would be better to say nothing to any one else about it until he was ready to act."

"Oh, of course," admitted Mollie. "The fewer the outsiders are who know about the—well, let's call them 'apples,' and then no one will suspect. The fewer who know about the 'apples' so much the better. But I do hope we each get one—'apple'—out of it," and she laughed.

"We ought to," returned Betty. She looked back toward the sand dunes, possibly for a sight of the old fishwife, but no one was in view.

The girls wandered on. The day was bright and beautiful, giving little hint of the tragic occurrence that was in the air. It was as if the outdoor girls were on one of the walking tours which they had instituted. The sand, however, was not conducive to rapid progress, and they were content to stroll idly.

They were now past the place where the diamonds had been found, though they were all anxious for a sight of the hole in the sand, to see if they could discover any signs that those who hid the precious stones there had come back to find their booty gone. But they did not think it wise to visit the place, with that queer old woman in the nearby sand dunes.

Now and then they would stop to pick up some prettier shell than usual, or to gather a few of the odd-shaped pebbles.

"They look just like that queer candy they sell in Tracey's," commented Grace, as she rattled a handful of the little stones of various colors, shapes and sizes.

"Oh, the pebble candy—yes," assented _Mollie_. "I wonder what they will imitate next?"

"Plenty of wood here for a marshmallow roast," commented Amy, a little later, as she idly kicked the bits of drift on the beach.

"Yes!" exclaimed Grace. "But we didn't bring any. I meant to, but——"

"She had so much other candy she couldn't carry marshmallows," interrupted Betty.

Grace threw a wisp of seaweed at her chum, but the Little Captain easily dodged it.

"I wonder if Percy will really come for us in the car?" asked Amy, after a pause.

"Do you want him to?" asked Betty, with a smile.

"I? No, indeed!" and Amy's face was suffused with a blush.

"Oh, well, don't get fussy about it," mocked Mollie. "We don't want him, either."

"He'd have trouble running his car through this sand," Grace said. "It's awfully deep and dry. Let's stop. When are we going to eat?"

"Eat?" cried Mollie.

"Eat?" echoed Amy. "Why we just had breakfast!"

"Eat?" spoke Betty, in a tone characterized as "dull and hopeless," in stories. "Why, Grace Ford, if you have done anything else but eat—candy—ever since we started on this picnic, I'd like to know it!"

Poor Grace looked a little startled at this combined attack on her.

"Why, I—I haven't done anything," she said, innocently enough. "I just asked when you were going to eat and you take me up as though I had proposed throwing those—'apples'—we found, into the sea."

"If you look back along the way you'll see at least three empty candy bags," declared Betty.

"Oh, well, they were little bags," protested Grace. "I had them put in small bags on purpose so I would know just how much I was eating."

"I don't believe you ever know how much candy you are eating," laughed Mollie. "Never mind, Grace, we all have our faults."

"We'll eat soon," promised Betty. "I want to get in the shade."

They strolled on, walking near the wet edge of the sand where the tide was coming in, for that section of the beach made firmer footing.

"There's a good place for our picnic," finally decided Mollie, as she saw a little clump of scrub evergreens which grew rather close to the water. "We can eat and have a fine view at the same time."

"Is that the boys' boat out there?" asked Mollie, as they made their way toward the bit of shade.

"No, that's a small schooner. It's been anchored there for some days," Betty said. "There's something queer about it, too."

"Something queer?" repeated Amy.

"Yes, the men in it don't seem to be gathering clams, which work all the other schooners are engaged in around here, and they're not net fishermen aboard her."

"Who told you that?" asked Mollie.

"Old Tin-Back. He notices anything odd about the boats. He said he passed her in his dory the other day, and some one yelled to him not to come too close."

"Why was that?" Grace asked.

"That's what Tin-Back didn't know. He thought it was very strange," Betty went on. "But come on, I know Grace must be—famished! Aren't you, my dear?"

The baskets were opened, and the contents spread out on a cloth on the sand. Grace reached for the bottle of olives.

"For an appetizer," she explained.

"You need it, after munching candy all the way here," commented Mollie.

And then, as they ate, the girls talked of many matters, now and then looking off toward the bay or ocean, whereon could be seen many vessels, mostly little clamming schooners, drifting with the wind on their squared sails, dragging the big rakes along the bottom. But the schooner of which Betty had spoken rose and fell at her anchor, and there was no sign of life aboard.

"This is just perfect," remarked Grace, as she found a comfortable position, leaning back against a tree. "Please don't disturb me, any one, I'm going to sleep."

"I believe I'll join you," added Mollie. "Salt air always makes me drowsy. Or perhaps it is the effect of the bright sun on the sand."

While Mollie and Grace closed their eyes, Betty dug idly in the sand, and Amy produced a handkerchief and a tiny embroidery frame and began initialling a corner.

"Virtuous girl," observed Betty. "You shame us all by your industry."

"It's only that I promised Henry I would put his initials on some new handkerchiefs he bought," Amy explained. "I must hurry and finish them, for he is going West on a trip soon."

"It's nice to have a brother," remarked Betty, idly.

She tossed some sand and little pebbles toward Grace, but the latter had actually gone to sleep, and the deep and regular breathing of Mollie proclaimed the same fact.

"Oh, I can't stand this!" the Little Captain cried, a few minutes later. "I want to do something. Let's go for a little walk, Amy, and let them sleep."

"All right."

"Will you go as far as the place where we found the—'apples'?" asked Betty, with a look around to be sure no stray fishermen were in the neighborhood.

"Yes, if you like."

"Then come on. I want to see if the men came back, and tried to find the box that was buried in the sand."

It was rather a longer walk than Betty had thought, but finally she and Amy came within sight of the lone fisherman's hut, and the log that lay on the edge of the hole in the sand, though the latter, so Betty expected, would be filled up by the action of the waves or wind ere this.

"I do hope that horrid old woman doesn't invite us in again," Betty remarked. "She is a—pest!"

The Little Captain and Amy were walking down the sands, in the midst of a number of high dunes, or hills.

"There's the place!" Betty said. "It doesn't seem to have been——"

A noise behind caused her to turn suddenly. A scream came to her lips, but it was choked off by the sudden forward rush of the old crone who roughly placed her withered hand over Betty's mouth.

"I—I've got her!" she croaked. At the same time a man caught Amy by the arm, and stifled her impending cry in the same manner.

THE OLD CRONE PLACED HER HAND OVER BETTY'S MOUTH.—Page 162.

The Outdoor Girls at Ocean View.

CHAPTER XXI

ON THE SCHOONER

Betty Nelson was an unusually muscular girl. She and her outdoor chums had not lived so much in the open air for nothing, and taken long tramps and regular physical exercise. They had played basketball, tennis and golf, and though their arms looked pretty in evening dresses, there were muscles beneath those same beautifully tanned skins.

For a moment Betty was so surprised at the suddenness of the attack that she could do nothing. She had had but a momentary glimpse of the face of the old crone, and only for that she might have thought it was the boys, who had stolen up behind her and Amy, and had put their hands over their eyes to make them guess who had thus blinded them.

But in an instant Betty knew this was no friendly game. And so, as soon as she realized that, she began to struggle, and to some good purpose.

She managed to pull from her mouth the horrible, fishy-smelling hand of the old woman, and then Betty screamed as she endeavored to loosen the grip the old crone had on her arms.

"Help! Help!" screamed Betty. "Let me go! How dare you! What does this mean? Amy, where are you?" for Betty could not, for the moment, see her chum.

But poor Amy was not as muscular as Betty, nor did she have the advantage of battling against a woman, for a man had caught her, and held her in a cruel grip.

"Help! Help!" Betty cried again, struggling desperately.

"Be quiet! Be quiet, my little dear—little imp!" hissed the old woman, for Betty had struck her in the face. "Be quiet or I'll——"

"Can't you stop her screams?" roughly demanded the man. "She'll have some one buzzing down on us if you don't! Clap a stopper on her, or I'll——"

"You must be quiet, my dear!" hissed the old crone, struggling to infuse some measure of conciliation in her cracked voice. "Be quiet or——"

"I'll not! Let me go! How dare you! Help! Help!" screamed Betty, but, even as she called, she realized how hopeless it was, for she saw no one in sight and the thunder of the surf would not permit her cries to carry far. She tried to get a sight of Amy, but could not.

"Let me—let me——" panted Betty, and then, though she struggled with all her might, making the old woman pant and hiss to overcome her, Betty found herself being gradually exhausted. Again that horrid hand stole over her mouth, making her feel ill, and effectually shutting off her cries.

"Quick!" panted the old woman. "I can't hold her much longer. You'll have to tie her—or—something."

"I'll do *something*, all right!" said the man, significantly. He was having little trouble with poor Amy, who had yielded like some broken flower. "I'll just tie this one up, and then take care of her," the fellow went on.

Betty had a glimpse of his dark and brutal face and she shuddered. It was bad enough to have him touch Amy, and bad enough for the old fishwife to clasp Betty in her horrid arms, but Betty thought she surely would die if that man approached her.

She tried to speak—to say that she would not scream again if they would only tell what they wanted—take her purse and its contents—but only let her alone. But she could only mutter a meaningless jumble of sounds with that fishyhand over her mouth, pressing cruelly on her lips.

"Can you carry her, and keep her from screaming?" asked the man, who had pulled some cords from his pocket and was quickly tying Amy's hands. Then he fastened a rag over her mouth, and poor Amy, who came out of a half-faint, was too late to add her voice to Betty's.

"Carry her—no, she'll struggle like a cat!" muttered the old woman. "You'll have to help."

"Help! Haven't I got my hands full?" he demanded. "Where are some of the others? They ought to be back now. They knew this chance might come any time."

"They have been lying in wait for us," thought Betty. It was one of the many ideas that raced through her brain at express-train speed. "That is why this old woman wanted us to come to her hut."

"There's some one now!" exclaimed the man, leaning up from having put a cord around Amy's ankles as she lay on a sand hill.

"If it isn't some one she's brought by her yells," snarled the fishwife.

"No, it's Jake, thank goodness!" muttered the man, as a rough-looking specimen, the counterpart of himself, peered around a dune. "Get busy here, Jake, and truss up that other—cat!" the first man ordered.

"All right, Pete," was the answer. "Got any rope?"

"Here's some," and the one addressed as Pete kicked over some net-cord toward the newcomer.

Meanwhile Betty had desisted from her struggle to get loose. She was strong and wiry, but the old crone was more than a match for the Little Captain. The fisherman's wife seemed to know how to handle struggling persons, for she held Betty in a peculiar grip that was most effective. Bend and strain as Betty might, she could not break away, and that hand was still held over her mouth, preventing any further outcry.

"Just a minute now, Mag, and I'll have her safe," went on Jake, as, with practiced hands he whipped several coils of cord around Betty's wrists and ankles.

"Stop! Stop!" she implored as the woman's hand was taken from her mouth for a second. It was poor Betty's last chance to appeal, for, an instant later, a fold of ill-smelling cloth was put over her lips, and she was effectually gagged. Tears of shame, rage and fear came into her eyes.

"Now you can carry her, without any trouble," announced Jake, rising.

"Take 'em up to the shack," ordered Pete. "Then tell the others to get the boat ready."

Betty wondered what that meant. Were they to be kidnapped? She tried to look at Amy, but could not see her just then.

A moment later she felt herself being lifted up between the two men. It was useless to struggle.

Amy was much lighter than Betty, and was hoisted up to the shoulder of the old crone, who seemed wonderfully strong.

"Take a look out, Mag, and see if any one's in sight before we make a dash for the shack," directed Pete. "Her screams may have been heard. She yelled like a banshee!"

The fishwife, carrying the limp figure of Amy, peered beyond the line of sand dunes.

"No one in sight," she muttered, beckoning the others to advance.

"But what gets me is where the other two are," growled Pete who, with Jake, was carrying Betty. "There's four of 'em, and they've always been together ever since they come down here. Where are the other two? That's what I'd like to know."

Betty shuddered as she thought of Mollie and Grace sleeping in the little clump of trees. Suppose these horrid men should go back there and find them. It was horrible to contemplate.

"Well, you've got half of 'em. That ought to be enough for what you want," said Jake, hoarsely chuckling.

Betty was puzzling her brains, trying to think why she and Amy had been thus captured. What object had the old fisherman and, too, why had the old crone been so eager to get them to her hut? Betty could only guess. Her head ached. She felt really ill, and could not doubt but that poor Amy was in like condition.

A few seconds later they were both carried into the hut, and set in rickety chairs. Their bonds were not removed, and the door was closed and locked. Amy looked over at Betty, and the latter could see that her chum's eyes were filled with tears.

Then, suddenly, Amy seemed to collapse. She slipped from the chair to the floor.

"Now what's up?" roughly demanded Pete. "I wish I'd never gone into this girl business, anyhow—it's so uncertain. What's happened?" and he looked at the limp form of Amy on the floor.

Betty tried to rise, but sank back dizzily. The room seemed to become suddenly dark. She feared she would topple over as Amy had done.

"It's only a faint, the poor dear," chuckled the old woman. "I'll attend to her. You go out and get the boat ready," she told the two men.

Betty's brain became clearer. There was no longer blackness before her eyes.

"Here, drink this," said the woman, raising Amy by her shoulders, and holding a glass of water to her lips. The gag had been removed. Amy drank and a little color came into her face.

"Where—where am I? What happened?" she faltered.

"Nothing, dearie," said the hoarse voice of the crone. "You'll be all right soon. You're just going to stay with me a little while—you and your friend. You won't suffer a bit of harm, if you tell us what we want to know. You'll be well taken care of."

Betty began to see a light now. She wished the gag might be taken from her lips, and water given her, but the old woman was busy with Amy. The girl closed her eyes again, and seemed too weak to cry out, even though the rag was not again bound across her lips.

There sounded voices outside the cabin, and a knock on the door.

"Drat 'em," muttered the old woman. "A body would need four hands to attend to all that's to be done."

She laid Amy back on the floor, and hobbled across the room to unbar the door. Betty was frantically struggling to loosen the bonds that held her hands behind her back.

"The boat's ready," gruffly said Jake, as he and Pete were admitted to the shack.

"That's good," muttered the old crone. "We can take care of 'em easier when we get 'em out of here. We don't care if they do yell then. Wait until I tie up this one's mouth. She may rouse up enough to make a racket."

Poor, half-senseless Amy was again gagged. Betty had given up trying to loosen her bonds. Those men knew how to tie knots.

And then, as before, Betty was carried down to the shore and placed in a boat. Amy was brought down on the shoulders of the old woman, who also got in the boat with the captured girls.

"Now row out," she ordered the man. They were on the bay side, where there was no surf, so the boat was easily pushed out. The men leaped in and began pulling on the long oars. Betty could see them heading for the mysterious schooner, and, a little later she and Amy were lifted on board that vessel.

"Up anchor!" came the command from some one, and, an instant later, the vessel was in motion.

Poor Betty wished she could do as Amy had done, and faint.

CHAPTER XXII

THE SEARCH

Grace Ford slowly opened her eyes. Grace seldom did anything in a hurry, not even awakening, and on this occasion, after the little doze that hot summer day, in the grove by the seashore, she was even more dilatory than usual in bringing all her faculties into play.

Lazily enough she glanced over at Mollie, who was still asleep. Grace felt a little sense of elation that she was awake before her friend. She did not look around for Betty or Amy, but, picking up a small pebble, tossed it in Mollie's direction.

Straight and true it went, alighting on the sleeper's nose, which, in spite of the assurance of her friends, Mollie felt was always likely to be classed as "slightly pug."

"Score one for me!" laughed Grace, still lazily, as Mollie sat up with a start. There was nothing slow about Mollie, waking or sleeping.

"What is it? Oh, you! Did you throw that?" she asked, rubbing her nose, on which a little red spot had been raised. Feeling a sting there Mollie opened her bag and gave a hasty glance at the little mirror hidden in one flap.

"You mean thing!" she cried. "And you know how sensitive my skin is!" By this time Mollie had glanced around her, something which Grace had not yet done.

"Why—why," Mollie exclaimed. "Where is Betty—and Amy?"

"Oh, probably off somewhere indulging in athletic stunts for fear they'll lose their figures on account of eating so much lunch," remarked Grace, reaching out her hand toward a box that had held some chocolate almonds.

"But they're not in sight!" declared Mollie. She rose to her feet, and glanced rapidly up and down the beach. "I can't see them anywhere," she went on. "They—could they have gone back and left us sleeping here?"

"Well, we certainly were sleeping," admitted Grace, with a smile that was lazy—like her drawling words.

"Oh, do be sensible—for once!" exclaimed Mollie, and her tones had a snap to them that made Grace sit up and fairly gasp.

"Why, whatever is the matter, Billy?" she asked in aggrieved accents. "I haven't done anything. And just because Betty and Amy aren't here——"

"That's just it—where are they?" asked Mollie, sharply.

"How should I know?" returned Grace, determined not to be conciliated so easily. "They went off for a walk while we were asleep, I suppose."

"Yes, but unless they went a long distance we ought to be able to see them," Mollie went on. "And they're not in sight—you can see for yourself."

"If they're not in sight I *can't see*, Mollie dear," spoke Grace, this time soothingly.

"Oh, do be sensible!" snapped the other. "Stop eating that silly candy, and help me gather up some of these things. I—I wonder what could have happened?"

The manner in which Mollie said this startled Grace as perhaps nothing else could have done.

"Help me up," she begged. "This skirt is so narrow. Oh, Mollie, do you think——" and she paused with frightened eyes, gazing into the more determined ones of her chum.

"I don't know that I think anything—just now," replied Mollie, in rather gentler tones. "I'm afraid I was a bit cross, Grace, but you know, dear it is——"

"A *bit* cross! You were positively—horrid. But I forgive you."

"I'm always cross when I wake up suddenly," explained Mollie. "You shouldn't have hit me on the nose, Grace."

"I wouldn't have, had I known you were such a—er—what animal is it that has such a sensitive nose, Mollie?"

"Bear, I guess you mean," Mollie admitted.

"Yes, that's it. Oh, but I did have a nice sleep!" and Grace lazily stretched first one arm and then the other. "But where are Betty and Amy keeping themselves?" she asked.

"That's just what I've been trying to get you to realize," said Mollie. "It's rather strange of them to go so far away."

"Oh, probably Betty wants to get some more shells for those string portiers she is making," Grace said. "Come on, we'll walk down the beach a little way ourselves."

Mollie assented and the two were soon strolling down the strand, looking in advance for a sight of their chums.

But the seashore was deserted, save for the presence of some birds that swooped down now and then to snap up the hopping white insects which made such queer little burrows down in the sand.

A few hundred feet beyond the little grove where the picnic had been held, Mollie and Grace came to a pause.

"I don't see them," Mollie said, and her voice was troubled.

"Nor I," conceded Grace. "Do you suppose they can be hiding to play a joke on us?"

"They might," Mollie admitted. "But they would hardly go so far away."

"Let's look on the other side," proposed Grace. But that beach, of the little arm of land that jutted out into the bay and ocean, showed no sight of Betty and Amy.

"Oh, I—I'm getting—worried," returned practical Mollie. "Nothing could have happened, unless one of them sprained her ankle, or something like that, and can't walk. Even then the beach is so open, and there isn't a place on it that one need fear——"

"Unless it's that old fisherman's hut," broke in Grace.

"Oh," observed Mollie, slowly, and there came a change over her face. "I didn't think of that. Yes, they might——"

She was interrupted by a shrill whistle, as if of some boat. Both girls turned quickly, and the same exclamation came to the lips of both.

"The boys!"

It was the *Pocohontas* approaching, and Allen, Roy and Henry waved their hands as they came on swiftly over the blue waters.

"Are they in the boat?" asked Grace.

"Who?" Mollie wanted to know.

"Betty and Amy."

"Why, how could they be?"

"I thought perhaps the boys might have come up while we were asleep, taken Betty and Amy out for a little run, and were now coming back, to laugh at us for being so lazy."

"Well, they're not in the motor boat, anyhow," Mollie said. "I do hope nothing has happened."

Grace did not ask what might possibly have happened. She was just a little afraid of what her chum might say. The sprained ankle theory was too simple. Somehow Grace felt a growing concern.

But, for the present, at least, this was lost sight of in the little excitement over the advent of the boys. They came on, laughing, singing and shouting, while Roy held up a string of fish. Evidently they had had good luck.

The motor boat grounded gently in the shallow water and the boys jumped out, Allen tossing out a light anchor high up on the sand.

"We came to take you home," he announced. "We thought you'd have enough of picnic by this time. Where's Betty?" he asked, quite frankly. Allen was not at all fussy about showing his admiration for the Little Captain.

"Why, it's queer," Mollie replied, smiling just the least bit, "but she and Amy seem to have gone off by themselves. Grace and I dozed, and when we awoke they were gone."

"Probably down the beach," suggested Roy. "How's that for fish?" and he held up the string. But Mollie and Grace were not interested in fish just then.

"We've been looking for them," Mollie went on. "We were looking when—when you came."

Something in her words and manner caused Allen to ask quickly:

"You—you don't think anything could have happened; do you?"

"I—I don't know what to think," Mollie faltered. "It seems—a little strange."

"Oh, we'll find them," declared Henry. "Amy isn't one to go far."

"But Betty is a great walker," Grace ventured.

"Well, we'll find them and all go back in the boat," proposed Allen. "It looks as though we might have a thunder shower. That's why we gave up fishing. Come on, have a look."

It did not take a very long search up and down the beach to disclose the fact that Amy and Betty were nowhere near. The little clump of trees held no hiding place, and unless they had gone inland there was no other explanation except that they had gone back to the cottage.

"And this they would hardly do," said Mollie. "Unless something had happened. Maybe——"

"What?" asked Roy, as she stopped suddenly.

"Oh, nothing," she said in some confusion. "Nothing at all."

"They may have gone over to that fisherman's hut, just to see what it was like," Mollie said. "You know the old woman was always teasing us to come in and have some milk. She may have been more persuasive this time, though Betty couldn't bear her."

"We'll have a look in that direction," suggested Henry.

"Yes, for I don't just like the looks of the weather," added Allen. "Henry and I will go over there," he said. "Roy, you stay here with the girls and help them pack up the things. We may have to make a run for it when we come back with Betty and Amy."

"If you find them," said Mollie, in a low voice—so low that no one heard her.

Allen and Henry set off over toward the sand dunes behind which was hidden the fisherman's shack. Grace, Mollie and Roy began collecting the picnic things.

The young law student and his chum made good time. Nor did they waste any when they reached the lone cabin. A glance up and down the beach showed no trace of the missing ones. In the offing a schooner was slowly sailing away.

"There goes that boat," remarked Allen. "Didn't seem to have any business around here—neither clamming or fishing."

"That's right," agreed Henry. He knocked, and, after waiting a moment, tried the latch. The door swung open, showing the place to be deserted.

"Betty—Amy!" called Allen.

There was no answer. Then with a quick motion Henry darted forward and picked up something from the floor. It was a handkerchief.

"It's my sister's," he said. "They—they've been here!"

He and Allen looked at each other strangely.

CHAPTER XXIII

SMUGGLED DIAMONDS

Slowly the mysterious schooner gathered headway. Her sails creaked and groaned as the ropes slipped through the sheaves, and the chains squeaked around the drum of the steering wheel. There was a rattle of blocks, hoarse cries from several sailors on deck, and then, down in the cabin, where the horrid old woman slipped the pieces of cloth from the mouths of Betty and Amy, had the two girls the strength to utter cries it is doubtful if they would have been heard a hundred feet away.

There was no other craft within a mile of the vessel that was moving up the bay toward the more open water.

"There you are, my dear," leered the fishwife. "All nice and snug and comfortable."

"Oh—oh!" gasped Betty, as the creature stretched out her hands toward her. "Don't—don't you dare touch me!"

"Jest goin' to take the ropes off your pretty hands, dearie," was the smirking answer. "You don't need them now. You can't run away, you know. Tee-hee!" and she tittered in glee.

Betty felt it better to submit to the ministrations of the crone, for the sake of being released from the bonds, which hurt her cruelly. For they had been pulled tight by the fishermen. It was some time after the ropes were taken off her ankles and wrists before Betty felt the blood circulating normally.

176

Amy lay inert on the rude bunk where she had been placed. Betty noticed there were sleeping accommodations for three in the place, and with a shudder she wondered if the old woman was to be their companion on the voyage that seemed to have begun. For the schooner was pitching and tossing on a ground swell, that seemed to presage a change of weather.

"Oh—oh, Betty! What has happened?" faltered Amy, as she opened her eyes. The cloth had been removed from her mouth and the ropes loosed. Having done this much the old woman crouched on the third bunk, smiling, muttering to herself, and looking from one girl to the other.

"Oh, Betty—what does it mean?" repeated Amy.

"I don't know, but I'm going to find out soon," declared the Little Captain, with a return of her usual courage. She felt better now that she had the use of her arms and legs. She started toward the door.

"It's locked—on the outside, my dearie!" chuckled the old woman. "And it won't be opened until I call to 'em. So there's no use in makin' a fuss, my dear!"

"Stop your senseless talk!" snapped Betty. "Don't dare call me by that name, you—you horrid creature."

"No use gettin' mad," said the crone, and she showed a change of temper. "You're here, and you're goin' to stay until we put you on shore, so you might as well make up your mind to that."

"We demand to be put on shore at once!" cried Betty. "Evidently you and—and those with you have made some mistake. We will not make trouble for you, if you set us ashore at once. If not——"

"Well, what will you do, dearie?" sneered the old woman.

"My father will deal with such as you!" declared Betty, her eyes flashing. "You must put us ashore."

"The men will have to attend to that," the crone said. "One of 'em will be here pretty soon, and you'd better answer 'em fair, or it may be the worse for you."

Her tone was fierce now.

"Oh—oh, I—I feel faint," gasped Amy. "It is so close in here——"

"Get her some water," ordered Betty, authoritatively.

"It's right here," said the old woman. "I thought you'd want a drink. And you can have somethin' to eat as soon as you like. It sha'n't be said we starved you."

"Eat! I couldn't bear the sight of food!" said Betty, with a shudder. "Here, Amy, drink this. It seems to be—clean!" and Betty tried to express the contempt she felt for the slovenly appearance of the old woman.

Fortunately the water did seem to be drinkable, and it was quite cold, as though it had been on ice. Both girls drank gratefully, for their mouths were parched and dry.

"Are you better?" asked Betty, smoothing back the hair of her chum.

"Oh, yes, much. But, Betty dear, what does it all mean? Why are we here? I—I seem to be in a sort of daze."

"I feel that way myself. I don't know what has happened, Amy, except that we were kidnapped, and brought to this schooner."

"Kidnapped? Oh, no, my dear!" interrupted the old woman. "We only want you to tell us something, and as soon as you do that you can go where you please."

"Tell you? Tell you what?" demanded Betty, though she felt she could answer that question herself.

"I don't rightly know what it is, my pretty!" protested the crone with an evil glance. "My man will be here pretty soon and tell you. He has to get the sails up, and all of that, first."

The creaking of pulleys on the deck told that the operation of getting the schooner under way was not yet completed. There was a regular swing to the vessel now, however, that told she was getting into more open water. Fortunately both the outdoor girls were good sailors.

The old woman was putting back in a box the bottle of water and the tin cup from which she had given Amy and Betty to drink. For a moment her back was turned, and Betty decided on a bold move.

Quickly she darted over toward the door, and pulled with fierce strength on the knob. It resisted her efforts. The old woman turned with a mocking smile on her wrinkled face.

"I told you it was locked," she jeered. "It won't be opened until I knock in a certain way. I'll do it soon, for we must be getting pretty well out."

She peered through a dirty round window that gave light to the cabin, which seemed to be located in the after part of the schooner, though neither Betty nor Amy had noticed to which part they had been taken.

"I demand that you let us out of here!" cried Betty, stamping her foot.

She looked around as though for some weapon with which to enforce her orders, and the woman evidently guessed this, for she chuckled grimly.

"You can't have your own way here," she said, with a grin that showed her almost toothless gums. "My man is captain of this boat, and out at sea, you know, the captain has to be obeyed."

"Oh, are you going to take us out to sea?" gasped Amy. "Please don't! I'll do anything if you will release us. See, I have money," and she brought out a little gold purse from a skirt pocket. At the sight of the gleaming metal the crone's eyes glittered.

"Don't be afraid," she said. "You won't be harmed. All we want to know is——"

A knock interrupted her. She glided quickly between Betty and Amy and the door was opened a crack. Betty had a wild idea of forcing her way out, but she had a glimpse of two rough looking men through the opening, and she darednot approach. There was a whispered talk between the old woman and one of the men.

Then, in an instant the old crone slipped out, and the door was locked again, leaving Betty and Amy alone in the cabin.

"Oh—oh!" cried Amy, and a moment later she was sobbing in the strong arms of Betty.

Meanwhile Allen and Henry had come out from the fisherman's cottage, having satisfied themselves, by a quick search, that no one was in the upper story, or down in the cellar.

"They were here, though," Allen said.

"Yes, my sister's handkerchief proves that," agreed his chum. "Now we must go back to the others."

"But Grace and Mollie will have a fit when they know we haven't found Betty and Amy."

"It can't be helped. There has been some mix-up somewhere. I have an idea, but I won't spring it now. Come on."

They hurried back to where the motor boat had been left.

"Were they there?" asked Grace, eagerly.

"Yes, they—were," said Allen, slowly. "But they've gone home."

"How do you know that?" asked Henry in a low voice.

"I don't know it!" came the reply in a whisper. "But we've got to pretend that until we find it isn't so. I'm hoping it is, though. You see," he went on, aloud, "we found they had been there. Amy dropped her handkerchief."

"But where are they now?" demanded Mollie.

"They probably hurried back to the cottage."

"But without coming to tell us?" objected Grace.

"They probably had no time," said Allen. "My idea is," he went on, speaking rapidly so he would not be interrupted, "that they got some news about the diamonds, and had to act on it quickly. I think that is why they didn't wait to tell you girls. They knew if they didn't come back that you would know enough to come home, or they may have planned to return to you later."

"What had we better do?" asked Grace.

"Get back to Edgemere as soon as we can," was Allen's opinion. "We'll probably find them waiting for us."

They piled into the motor boat, and used all speed in getting back. No sooner had they reached the little dock, where Tin-Back tied his boats, than Will Ford came racing down from the cottage.

"I thought you would never come back!" he cried, his face showing excitement.

"Why, have you found them? Are they here?" asked his sister, wondering why her brother had returned from Boston.

"Here? Of course they're here!" he answered. "Where else would they be. And I've found them."

"I don't see how——" began Allen.

"Oh, it wasn't easy, I assure you. I had to work on a lot of clues. But I came out all right. I've found out all about 'em. Those diamonds were smuggled, and there's a good reward offered for the capture of the men, as well as something due for turning the diamonds over to Uncle Sam."

"The diamonds!" cried Mollie.

"Yes. I've found out their secret!" Will said.

"We—we thought you meant you had found Betty and Amy," returned Grace, in a strange voice. "They—they're lost! They're gone!"

CHAPTER XXIV

TO THE RESCUE

"What gone? Not the diamonds!" cried Will, hopping about, first on one foot, and then the other. "Don't tell me those sparklers are gone, after all the trouble I've had on this case—and it's my first, too! That's a shame! How did it happen."

"Oh, you and your diamonds!" cried Allen. "It's the girls who are missing! Don't you understand? The girls!"

"I don't understand," replied Will. "What's the game?"

"And Betty and Amy are not up at the cottage?" asked Mollie.

Will shook his head.

"I just came down from Boston," he said. "I was told you were all out—the boys fishing and the girls on a picnic. I could hardly wait until you came back to tell you the news. But you've knocked my feet from under me."

"Oh, it's just terrible!" said Grace. "What will Mrs. Nelson say?"

"Now look here!" exclaimed Allen, taking charge of matters in the masterful way he had. "We've got to do something in a hurry. Of course Mrs. Nelson will have to be told, but it may be all right after all. Betty and Amy may have gone in to the village, to send a telegram, or something like that."

"What about?" asked Grace.

"The diamonds, of course. They may have struck a clue. Now look here," Allen went on quickly. "Will, as I understand it, you have found out to whom those stones belong?"

"Well, yes; that is, almost. There's been a big smuggling job, and those diamonds are part of the loot, or swag——"

"Such slang!" protested Grace.

"Don't worry about slang at a time like this," said Mollie. "Go on, Will."

"No, we haven't time for all his story now," said Allen. "It is enough for us to know that he has solved the mystery."

"This much of it, at any rate," Will assented, "though I'm in the dark yet about the missing girls. As I said, I've been working my government position for all it's worth. There was a big smuggling job lately, and they were keeping it quiet. These diamonds are undoubtedly part of it, and now if I can only help get some of the men it sure will be a feather in my cap—a whole ostrich plume, in fact."

"Well, the rest of your story will keep," Allen remarked. "The next thing is to trace the girls. Here's the story about them, Will," and he rapidly told it as he had gathered it from Mollie and Grace.

"At the fisherman's hut, eh?" mused Will. "I always thought he had a hand in the affair. But where did the girls go from there?"

"That's just what we don't know," Henry remarked. "I found Amy's handkerchief in the cabin, or we wouldn't have known that much."

"It's a bare chance that they may have gone to the telegraph office in the village, to send a wire to Betty's father," said Allen. "We'll try there before we raise an alarm."

"But can we keep the news from Mrs. Nelson?" asked Mollie.

"She isn't home," Will said. "She's out calling somewhere. I've been keeping bachelor's hall at Edgemere ever since I came from the train. The maids told me where you were."

"We might stave off worrying Mrs. Nelson if one of us could get to town and back before she returned," said Allen. "Of course if the girls haven't been there we'll have to come out with the whole story."

"If we only could get to the village in a rush," said Mollie.

"An auto!" exclaimed Grace.

"There isn't one near enough——" began Will, when Grace cried:

"Percy Falconer! There he comes!"

The Deepdale johnny was coming down the road in his powerful machine. With all his faults he had the car in his favor, though he was not a skilled driver, and seldom could get anyone to venture out with him.

"Hey, Percy! You're just in time!"

"Over here!"

"This way!"

"Got to get to town in a hurry!"

Thus called the boys and girls to him, and it is doubtful if Percy Falconer ever received such a warm welcome before, or since.

"Just the one we want to see," said Allen, getting into the car with Will. "We are in a hurry to get to the telegraph office."

"Some one ill?" asked Percy, looking at his wrist watch.

"No, but there may be if we don't hustle," Allen said. "To the telegraph office as fast as you can make it, Percy boy."

"And let Allen drive, if you don't mind, old man," put in Grace's brother. "You must be tired, and we don't want to be ditched."

"Oh, all right, of course. If you're in a rush," agreed Percy, good-naturedly, and he found a warmer place in the hearts of those who had hitherto cared little for him.

"After all, Percy isn't such a bad sort," remarked Roy, as he walked with Grace and Mollie up the drive leading to Edgemere.

"He came in very useful to-day, at all events," Mollie agreed. "I think I shall teach him that new aeroplane whirl in the hesitation he is so anxious to learn."

"Oh, a dance!" acclaimed Grace. "I'm just dying for one."

"There won't be any—if we don't find Betty," said Mollie, seriously enough.

"Oh, we'll find them!" declared Roy.

"I hope Mrs. Nelson stays away until—well, until the scare is either over, or until we have something to go on, in case—in case they are lost," commented Grace.

Betty's mother had not returned home when the auto, driven at break-neck speed by Allen, swung down the road again.

"What news?" asked Mollie, as the echo of the screeching brakes died away. But there was no need to ask. A look at the faces of Allen and Will told her what she wanted to know.

"They weren't there, and hadn't been," said Allen, slowly.

"Oh, but I say! What's it all about?" asked Percy.

"You'll know soon enough," Will answered in a low voice.

As they stood on the porch, a much-worried group of young people, Mrs. Nelson came back from her call.

There was no need for her to ask if anything was the matter. A glance told her that. But she met the emergency bravely. The girls told their story first—how they had awakened to find Betty and Amy gone. Then Henry told of finding the handkerchief in the hut, and lastly Will explained how he had found out that the diamonds were the booty of a smuggling plot.

"Well, we must get right to work," said Mrs. Nelson, and she proved herself a worthy mother of a worthy daughter. "I am sure nothing serious could have happened—no drowning, or anything like that. The only other explanation is, I think, along the lines suggested by Allen.

"Their disappearance must have something to do with the diamonds. It is possible they are following some suspect, and have had no chance to send back word. In that case they are all right. But we must search for them, and begin at the fisherman's shanty.

"We must also telegraph for Mr. Nelson. I'll go to town and do that. I'll also try to get him on the long distance telephone. Now, let me see. Some of you will come with me, others will go to the fisherman's cabin, and others will start a search along the beach, and notify the life saving station. We must neglect nothing."

"Isn't she splendid?" asked Grace of Mollie. "I feel better already."

"So do I."

There was a hasty consultation, and three parties were made up. Percy offered the use of his car, and Allen elected to go in it with Mrs. Nelson, to town. The others would go to the fisherman's shack and to the life saving station, though at this time of year there was only one man on duty. But he would know how to organize a corps of fishermen and clammers to make a search, if needed.

Mrs. Nelson returned from the village, after sending a telegraph message. She was unable to communicate with her husband by telephone.

"We had best follow them to the fisherman's cabin," said Allen. "That will be a sort of rallying point."

There they found all the young folks gathered, those who had been assigned the task of going to the life saving station having accomplished their errand, bringing back the message that soon a body of hardy men would be patrolling both beaches.

But it was Tin-Back who gave the real clue. He came up as they were making a second examination of the cabin, to discover some other evidence of the former presence of Betty and Amy there.

"The girls missin'!" exclaimed the old crabber. "Wa'al, there's only one place t' look fer 'em!"

"Where's that?" asked Mrs. Nelson. "Not—not——"

"No'm, they're not drowned, don't fear that, mum," said Tin-Back, with ready perception. "Nothin' like that could happen. They're off—there!"

He waved his hand toward where the mysterious schooner had been anchored.

"What makes you think so?" asked Allen, after the crabber had spoken of his belief, and mentioned the absence of the schooner as evidence.

"Because that vessel has been hanging around here on purpose to work off some such scheme as that! Take my word for it, the girls are aboard her. Pete and his woman Mag haven't gone off together for nothin'. The girls are on the *Spud*, and bad luck to her for a sneaky craft!"

"There's no time to lose!" he went on. "We've got to take after 'em, and locate her before nightfall. We need a fast boat——"

"The *Pocohontas* is in good trim!" interrupted Allen.

"The very thing!" cried Tin-Back. "Hurray! This is like old times! I'm with you!" and he clapped his hand on his thigh with a report like a pistol shot. "To the rescue!" he cried.

CHAPTER XXV

ALL'S WELL—CONCLUSION

"All aboard!"

It was the tense voice of Allen Washburn calling, as he and his chums clambered aboard the *Pocohontas*. There had been a hurried filling of the gasoline and oil tanks after the suggestion offered by Tin-Back, that the disappearance of the mysterious schooner was coincident with the disappearance of the girls.

"If she only will run," ventured Roy, who was in charge of the motor.

"She's *got* to run!" declared Allen, fiercely. Not all of the party went in the motor boat. Mrs. Nelson did not feel equal to the task, but Mollie said she would go, for her girl chums might need her in case they were found.

Tin-Back went, of course, with Henry, Allen and Roy. Will volunteered to stay with Mrs. Nelson and Grace. At first he had begged to be taken along, but some one had to stay to be the "man of the house," and I think, after all, Will wanted to get another look at the diamonds, in which he now had so strong and growing an interest.

"Let her go!" cried Allen, and the motor boat glided away from the little dock. It was late afternoon, and while the threatened storm had held off, the daylight was fast fading.

Fortunately they had a clue as to the direction the schooner had taken after leaving her anchorage. The man at the life saving station had observed her beating out on a long tack. He had noticed her through a glass, but had taken no note of any girls that might have been put aboard. But the wind was now quite strong, and the schooner would hardly sail against it. So our friends had a certain fairly sure direction to follow.

Will and Mrs. Nelson, with Grace and Percy, went back to the cottage. Their first care was to see that the diamonds were safe, and this was soon ascertained to be the case.

Meanwhile the motor boat had taken up the search. Driven at top speed, and with the engine "doing its prettiest," as Roy boasted, they made good time. In and out they went, over the course, now and then pausing to speak some clammer, but getting no information, save in one or two instances. But hey learned enough to know that they were on the right track.

"Are you going to cruise all night," asked Mollie.

"No, unfortunately we'll have to turn back at dark," Allen said. "That is why I want to cover as much water as possible before all the light is gone."

They chased after one or two schooners, but without result, until, just as the last light of a threatening day was fading, Tin-Back startled them all by leaping up and shouting:

"Sail, ho!"

"Where away?" demanded Allen, in true nautical fashion.

"Dead ahead. There she is or I'm a candidate for Davy Jones's locker! Put after her, boys!"

It was comparatively easy, for the wind had died out—the calm before a storm, and as the schooner had no "kicker," or small gasoline engine, as had some of the clammers, she was soon overhauled.

That she was at least the one which had been anchored out in the bay was evident, for Tin-Back recognized her at once. Also it was evident that no visitors were desired, for, as the *Pocohontas* came up alongside the almost motionless sailing craft, an ugly face looked over the low rail, and a gruff voice cried:

"That'll do, now. Keep off or you'll get into trouble! What do you want, anyhow?"

"You know well enough what we want!" cried Allen. "Up on deck, boys! We've got 'em just where we want 'em. There's your man, officer!" he called. It was pure "bluff," but it seemed to have its effect, for the man who had given the warning drew back.

"What is it?" demanded some one else, coming up out of the cabin.

"Oh, some fresh guys——"

"Come on, fellows!" Allen called loudly. He had leaped out on the forward deck of the motor boat. Mollie had been urged to stay in the little cabin, and did so. But it was evident there was to be no serious trouble—at least just yet.

"Come on!" cried Tin-Back, and at the sound of his resolute voice there was a surprised exclamation from the group of men on the schooner's deck.

"All aboard!" yelled the old clammer. "We've got 'em where we want 'em! Close-hauled! We'll holystone 'em an' slush 'em with hot tar if they give any trouble! Come on!"

Another instant and, despite his age and the crippling effects of rheumatism caused by exposure in all sorts of weather, Tin-Back had leaped to the schooner's deck. He was followed by Roy, Allen and a couple of sturdy fishermen, who had been picked up on the beach.

"Now, then, what do you fellows want?" demanded Pete, who was recognized as the fisherman of the lonely cabin.

"You know well enough what we want!" answered Allen resolutely. "The two young ladies you have on board here."

"There's nobody here," was the surly denial.

"I tell you there are!"

"You——"

There came a shrill scream from somewhere below decks, followed by an exclamation in a woman's voice.

"They're loose! They're loose. Pete—Jake—I—I——"

The men of the schooner uttered surprised exclamations.

195

"Come on!" cried Pete, leaping up.

"Not so fast," interposed Tin-Back, stepping in front of the man who had made a dash toward the cabin. "Wait a minute," and an extended foot tripped Pete, who fell heavily to the deck.

"We're coming!" shouted Allen, and, followed by Roy and Mollie, who by this time had made her way to the deck of the schooner, they hurried below. From behind a closed door came the sound of a struggle.

"In here!" cried Allen, and he threw himself against the panels as though he were stopping a rush on the football field. There was a cracking of wood and a snapping of metal. The door burst open.

In the cabin, struggling against the old crone, were Betty and Amy, disheveled and almost hysterical, but otherwise safe and sound.

"Allen!" gasped Betty, holding out her hands to him. He clasped them warmly, and the old crone, seeing that the whole affair was over, slunk off, whining something about meaning no harm to the "dearies"!

"Just watch those fellows that they don't do any mischief," said Henry to Tin-Back, when he had comforted his sister.

"Oh, they won't do any harm. They know it's all up. Besides, I brought this with me," and the clammer showed an ancient horse pistol, that, had it been fired, would probably have worked more havoc to the marksman than to the person aimed at.

There were tears, hysterical laughter, and rapid-fire explanations—all, seemingly, at once.

"But you're safe!" cried Allen, who had both Betty's hands. Whether or not it had been a continuous performance I cannot say. Probably it had. Betty was a very nice girl.

"Oh, yes, we're safe," she said, trying to control her voice.

"But those awful men; that—that horrid woman!" gasped Amy.

"You needn't worry about them any more," Allen assured her. "We'll see that they get what's coming to them."

Whether or not he would have been able to put this into operation is a question. But unexpected help arrived. It would not have been easy for the little force in the motor boat to cope with the larger crew of men on the schooner. Besides, there were three girls to be considered, and, though they were equal to most emergencies, both Betty and Amy were now rather unnerved.

There was a sharp whistle outside—a boat signal, evidently.

"What's that?" asked Allen, who, with Henry, Roy and the girls, was in the cabin, so recently a prison.

"It's a revenue cutter," bawled Tin-Back down the hatchway. "They want to know if we need help."

"We'll take it, anyhow," chuckled Allen. He felt like laughing now. "But how in the world did they come, and in the nick of time?"

"Maybe Will sent them," suggested Mollie. "They may be down here after the smugglers."

And so it proved when Allen went up on deck and held a short talk with an officer aboard the trim cutter, which had come to a stop alongside the motor boat and drifting schooner.

Will, left behind at the cottage with Mrs. Nelson and Grace, had suddenly thought to send the cutter *Minoa* to follow up the *Pocohontas*. The government vessel had come down to Ocean View in view of certain facts Will had given his chief in the Secret Service, but Will had not expected to use the *Minoa* in the chase. When he recalled that she was but a short distance off shore, awaiting wireless instructions, he rushed in Percy's auto to the telegraph office in town, and got into communication with his chief, who was awaiting word from him.

It was but the matter of a few minutes to relay the instructions to the cutter by wireless from Boston, and she started out to look for a small motor boat chasing a suspicious schooner. She found both in the nick of time.

Explanations made, men from the revenue vessel boarded the sailing craft and made her captain and crew prisoners, the old crone being among those captured. She had tried to make off in the rowboat trailing at the schooner's stern, but had been caught by Tin-Back.

"No, you don't!" he cried. "We want you!" and the old lobsterman held to her despite her struggles.

There were more explanations, and then, as the storm showed signs of breaking, the rescued girls and their friends set out for Ocean View in the motor boat. The revenue officers remained in charge of the captured schooner, and said they would see Will in the morning to complete the case.

"But what in the world did they want to capture you girls for?" asked Roy, when they were all safe again in Edgemere. The rain was beating against the windows, for they arrived just as the downpour began.

"They thought to get the secret of the diamonds," declared Will. "I can tell you that much. Though how they expected to do it I can't say."

"But were those men who had us—and that horrid old woman—the smugglers?" asked Amy.

"No, only their tools," Will said. "In brief, the game was this: The box of diamonds you found was smuggled from France. But before those interested in bringing them over could make good they received word that the customs officers in Boston were waiting for them. The government agents abroad had sent word here to be on the lookout.

"So the smugglers adopted a bold plan. They sent a message in cipher, by the ship's wireless, when two or three days outside of Boston, to their confederates, to have a boat waiting for them off this coast. That was done, and one dark night the smugglers tossed overboard the box with the diamonds concealed in the false bottom. It was fixed in a cork arrangement, so it would float. This box was picked up, but before the confederates could make away with it something happened. There was a quarrel among the smugglers, I believe, and one gang hurried off and buried the box here in the sand.

"You girls came along just as that had been done, and though some of the men wished to come back and take away the booty, others would not permit this, thinking no chance comer would find it."

"Those were the men we saw leaving in the boat," said Mollie.

"Yes," assented Will.

"And we did find the diamonds!" cried Grace.

"Yes, and that made all the trouble—for the smugglers," went on Will. "Of course they soon learned that the box was gone, and they guessed you girls had taken it. Then they tried to get it back."

"Those men in the cellar?" asked Betty

"Were part of the gang," declared Will. "And I learned that they found the diamonds were in the cellar because a tramp hanging around for food overheard us taking about them. He wasn't in with the smugglers then, but later he joined them, giving this information.

"But the plan to get the diamonds from the cellar failed, and they had to do something else. That old woman and her fisherman husband were delegated to capture one or more of you girls, and force you either to tell where the diamonds were, or else they were going to hold you as a ransom for them."

"How terrible!" cried Grace.

"But it's all over now," her brother said. "Now we have the diamonds, we have the poor dupes of tools the smugglers bribed—the fisherman and the men of the schooner—and it only remains to get the criminals themselves. We'll do it, too."

"Did they treat you badly?" asked Grace of Betty and Amy.

"Badly enough," the Little Captain replied. "They would not tell us why we were made prisoners. But after they had taken the gags from our mouths, they put them on again, just before you came."

"That was because they saw the motor boat after them and knew they couldn't get away because of no wind," suggested Will.

"We thought perhaps there was a pursuit," Amy said. "And then Betty grew desperate and managed to attack the old woman."

"But you helped," said Betty.

"Oh, don't let's talk about it," exclaimed Grace. "All's well that ends well."

"But it isn't all ended yet," Will remarked, significantly.

Working on the fears of their prisoners the government men learned where the real smugglers were hiding, waiting for the success of their plot, and they were arrested. In due time they were tried, found guilty and sentenced to pay heavy fines on the charge of trying to defraud Uncle Sam. On the charge of kidnapping the two girls the heavier punishment of imprisonment was meted out to those involved.

It developed that the smugglers, however, had protected themselves from the graver charge. They had instructed the fishermen to get information from the girls about the diamonds, in any way the ignorant men thought best, and the kidnapping scheme was the product of the brains of the old woman and her husband. They laid the plot to capture the girls, and secured the help of several friends, hiring the schooner for their purpose. When the schooner sailed away with Betty and Amy the old woman and her husband expected to pick up the smugglers and let them force the truth from the girls. But their plan was spoiled.

The diamonds, of course, became the property of the government, and were sold at auction, and on such favorable terms that each of the girls was able to obtain one for herself. Will helped bring this about, for the government was under obligation to him and his friends for recovering the jewels and capturing the smugglers. The reward was evenly divided.

"And I received a fine letter of thanks from my chief," said Will. "For my first case he said it was a—corker!"

"Oh, Will!" objected his sister.

"Well, he meant that, if he didn't say it," was the answer. "And I'm going to have a vacation which I'm going to spend down here if Betty will let me."

"Of course I will," she said. "We'll have jolly times!"

And then began glorious days at Ocean View, days in which there was no worriment about the packet of diamonds. Allen was allowed to keep the mysterious box and the original of the cipher, but he was never able to discover the meaning of it, nor who the enigmatical "B. B. B." was.

It was practically certain, however, that "B. B. B." was the real head of the smugglers, he who furnished the money and most of the brains. But his confederates never betrayed him. The value of the diamonds was several thousand dollars above Mr. Nelson's estimate.

There followed vacation days of boating and bathing, with more picnics, and Grace had all the chocolates she wanted—or at least all that were good for her. Tin-Back came in for a share of the reward, and bought himself, among other things, a new fish net.

And, while the outdoor girls are enjoying life at beautiful Ocean View, we will take leave of them.

The End

www.ingramcontent.com/pod-product-compliance
Lightning Source LLC
Chambersburg PA
CBHW070006300526
45794CB00001B/204